CREATING
Calm

How Understanding the Brain Can Transform
Stressful Situations into Peaceful Connections for
Educators and Parents

CHRISTINA RENZELLI

Copyright © 2020 by Christina Renzelli.

No part of this book may be reproduced, transmitted in any form, or stored in a retrieval system or by any means, photocopying, recording, electronic, mechanical or otherwise without prior written permission of the publisher. The publisher and author do not assume any responsibility for errors, omissions, inaccuracies, inconsistencies or contrary interpretation of this information. The events and conversations in this book have been set down to the best of the author's ability, although some names and details have been changed to protect the privacy of individuals. Any slights of people, places or organizations are unintentional. Therefore, this product should be used only as a general guide. The purchaser of this publication assumes full responsibility for the use of these materials and information.

Edited by Sarah Samuel

ISBN: 979-8-6775273-9-5

United States

Contact the Author: http://ChristinaRenzelli.com

First edition, first printing

To My kids and C.G.

*To Kamin Samuel and Sarah Samuel
for creating this book with me.*

*And, to Dr. Marion Bell for contributing
her insight and educational expertise.*

Contents

Why I Wrote This Book 1

Mya's Story 7

My Story As A New Teacher 13

The Effects Of Stress And Trauma 17

The Brain 31

How The Stress Response Works 37

The Effects Of Constant Dysregulation 53

Regulation 57

How To Create A Regulated Environment For Leaders 71

Empathy Is The Antidote To The Stress Response 79

Punishing Students For Trauma Responses Creates
More Stress And Trauma 83

Schools Can Transform Lives Or Crush Souls 91

Relationships Are Key 97

Taking Care Of Teachers 109

Creating Regulation Plans To Replace Punitive Systems 117

Conclusion 127

1
WHY I WROTE THIS BOOK

A thirteen-year old girl inspired me to write this book. I hope that I am able to tell her story in a way that makes a difference in our world. This young girl experienced a lot of toxic stress and trauma in her life, which caused her brain to be hypervigilant to potential threats. She would often react emotionally to perceived threats at school, which would cause her to be sent out of class and suspended.

This book is about the *stress response* and the way that trauma in our lives, especially during childhood, makes us react to stress. Not understanding the stress response can be at the root of much of our interpersonal conflict and communication problems. In schools, students are often punished for their stress response reactions by being suspended. Instead of working to solve the problem by teaching them the skills to self-regulate, students are sent home as punishment, where they may feel thrown out or abandoned. Instead, I believe we need to teach students and adults about the way their brains react to stress, and what to do about it. This empowers students; once they are aware and understand their reactions to stress, they are able to respond and self-regulate instead of reacting.

I wrote this book to show that unfair policies and practices can create stress and trauma by making people feel unsafe and threatened. It is my hope that the information in this book will improve institutions, organizations, and interpersonal interactions so that we can all understand the ways that stress and trauma impact our brains, bodies, health, society, and lives.

In order to change systems and structures that are inherently trauma-producing, we have to understand what happens in our brains and bodies when the stress response gets activated. I am not a brain expert, but I am a teacher and learning expert. I will share what I know about the stress response in the brain and how I have seen it play out practically so that we can better understand each other and ourselves and create more compassionate environments and relationships. I believe that if we can learn about how our brains work and respond to stress, we can learn how to self-regulate and have empathy for ourselves and others.

My experience as a teacher and a trauma-sensitive coach has been mostly in urban, inner-city schools and rural schools that have been low income and high trauma. The trauma that many students experienced in these schools was often related to generational poverty, racism, and generational trauma. I am sure that students in higher income schools experience trauma as well; it may just look different. This book will be based on my observations and experiences in low income, high trauma schools.

Obviously, understanding the stress response is only one piece of the puzzle. But I think it can be a place to start and a place to create some healing and change when it comes to interacting and connecting with each other. Understanding the stress response is one small step that could create a ripple effect, relationship by relationship.

This book is intended to show educators how to create trauma-sensitive learning spaces, reduce student behavior issues, increase learning, and empower students and teachers by teaching brain friendly self-regulation skills. This book sheds light on the issue of childhood trauma and the ways in which it can affect how our students respond to stress, creating higher reactivity to the fight, flight or freeze response. Trauma is at the root of many school problems, including behavior issues that lead to suspensions and missed school, classroom chaos, and teacher stress and burnout. This book will provide a blueprint for educators to transform their learning environments into safe, respectful, empowering spaces.

Most educators don't go into the field of education for the paycheck or summer vacation. We all know these are not real perks when you weigh the stress of the work and the toll that it takes on the mind and body. Educators go into teaching because we are called to serve students. And somewhere along the way, the educational system manages to suck the spiritual aspect out of it. Schools can be soul-crushing institutions, or they can be magical, creative, learning, nurturing wonderlands. We get to decide.

Our students bring unfathomable levels of trauma to school with them every day in the form of childhood neglect and abuse, incarceration of parents, divorce, racism, poverty, addiction, and many more disheartening life circumstances. For many of our students, childhood is a time just to figure out how to survive in a world that appears to be against them, and this has lasting impact on the brain, body, and emotional health. Our most vulnerable students are often retraumatized by the ways our school systems are set up. They are punished for their stress responses and misunderstood by teachers who have had inadequate training or lack awareness of the trauma they are experiencing. The students with the most trauma get branded as "the bad kids" and are pushed out of school by suspension and expulsions, furthering the likelihood that they will be retraumatized and re-punished, missing school and falling further behind both in their academics and spiritual morale. Students who have been suspended even once have a much higher likelihood of being incarcerated in their lifetimes. And when you see that the root of their original "misbehavior" was a misunderstood stress response, this fact becomes even more heartbreaking.

Teacher burnout is an epidemic because stress is contagious. Most teachers have not been adequately trained or prepared to understand the stress response that results from high levels of trauma. The high teacher turnover rates in high trauma schools means that our most vulnerable student populations usually have the most inexperienced teachers.

The truth is teachers can change lives. When teachers have the skills to connect with their students, especially the students who have experienced high levels of trauma and stress, the relationships between students and teachers can transform lives. Teachers have the opportunity to be the resilience builders that students need to get out of survival mode and thrive.

Understanding how common trauma is among children can change everything in a learning space. When we understand that most or all of our students have experienced some form of trauma, we can create spaces that are safe and respectful, avoiding re-traumatization. Schools can be terrifying for students who have experienced trauma. The high levels of uncertainty combined with the traditional power structures that focus on control rather than empowerment can trigger reactions of fight, flight or freeze, causing disruptions, fighting and perceived "disrespect."

In this book, we will learn:

- How to create a trauma sensitive learning environment. Optimally, the entire system would be transformed from the top, so that there is an organizational culture shift. When the entire system is aware of trauma and its prevalence and impacts, the entire organization will be transformed.

- How the brain's stress response works, how trauma creates a higher sensitivity to stress and trauma in everyday life, and how this impacts learning and student behavior issues.

- How to become more self-aware by understanding the stress response, stress contagion, and our own stress triggers so that we can stay regulated and reduce the risk of burning out, prevent energy drain, and improve wellbeing.

- How to self-regulate and teach students the skills they need to know to understand their own brains and stress response so that they will be empowered rather than stuck in their own survival mode.

- How to build strong relationships by cultivating empathy and connection.

- How to replace punitive systems of traditional schooling with brain friendly, trauma sensitive regulation plans.

Uncertainty and Virtual Learning

As teachers, parents, schools and students navigate the uncertainty of virtual learning and a pandemic, this information is more relevant than ever.

- Uncertainty in itself is a trigger for the stress response
- Children's brains need relationships with their peers, teachers and parents in order to develop; therefore this information is essential now more than ever.

2
MYA'S STORY

The following story is a compilation of situations that many of my students have told me they experience on a regular basis. My intent in creating this amalgamation is to paint a picture of some of the difficult situations our children face as a part of their daily lives. For the purposes of this story, I'll call the subject Mya.

<u>Imagine Mya's Morning</u>:

It is May 15th and the sun isn't up yet, but Mya is already in the kitchen preparing breakfast for her two younger sisters. This has been her routine for most of her seventh-grade year, ever since her baby brother was born in December. Smoke fills the air. Mya accidently burned the toast as she was scrambling the eggs.

Beyond the beeping of the smoke alarm, she hears the familiar sound of arguing begin. The stress of life with a newborn has caused additional friction in the already rocky relationship of Mya's mom and stepdad. As the argument heats up, the baby's cries get louder, until a thud creates a silence.

Mya shuttles her baby sisters into their bedroom, opens the window to clear the smoke, and with her heart pounding, goes in to check on her mother. She slowly cracks the door open, as smoke billows out. "Mom, are you ok?"

There's still silence as she pushes the door open. Her mother is on the floor, holding her bloody nose. The baby is in stepdad's arms as he bolts toward the door and curses at Mya to get the #$%^@! out and mind her own business.

Mya's mother insists that she is alright, but Mya knows she isn't ok. She hasn't really been ok since she met Mya's stepdad. He was hard to figure out. Sometimes he was nice to them, bringing them snacks and toys, playing and laughing. And other times, he was brutal – yelling, hitting and getting angry at the smallest of things.

The sight of blood panics Mya, and she starts toward her mother despite her stepdad's threatening presence, but her mother says, "I'm ok, just go and get your sisters and take them next door to the babysitter and go to school. I don't want you to be late again."

Mya goes to get her little sisters who are still under the bed where she had hidden them. She tries to turn on some false cheer, staying strong to protect them from the scary truth. Mya has become an expert at keeping her little sisters safe, calm, and happy. She created a "tent" for them underneath the bed a few months ago when everything had started to get worse. The tent was just a space under the bed that she had equipped with plenty of toys, soft cuddly stuffed animals, and a few snacks in case they had to stay put for a while. She knew what to do to protect them.

Her mom has a lot to handle, especially with the baby, and Mya is always there to help her. Her stepdad is the hot/cold type, meaning he is totally unpredictable in his behavior and moods. He drinks a lot and uses drugs. She never knows if he is going to talk to her with kindness or shout demeaning insults at her, calling her names she doesn't even understand the meaning of. The chronic unpredictability keeps her in a state of constant alarm as she remains vigilant for herself, her mother, and her sisters. After all, she is thirteen now, and in middle school. It is her responsibility as the oldest.

Mya takes her two little sisters next door to the babysitter and heads to school.

As she walks, some older men at the bus stop heckle her with obscenities, making vulgar comments about her body. She keeps her eyes down and moves straight ahead without flinching, as she has practiced many times before. "You little %$#*@, you can't even acknowledge us?" one of the men shouts, causing her to flinch imperceptibly.

This has become routine on her way to school. Men yell at her or sometimes whisper to her as she passes. And when she ignores them, they get angry and call her names.

She picks up her pace but refuses to run, even though that is her instinct. She can feel her heart pounding and her blood starting to boil as it rises, heating her cheeks in anger and fear.

She makes it to school just in time to pick up her breakfast from the cafeteria. As she gets in line, her heart feels jittery. Her stomach feels upset, but she didn't get the chance to eat at home after the burned toast and fighting and she knows she must eat something in order to sit through her classes all morning.

While in line, she hears some boys in front of her making inappropriate gestures and comments about some girls. They are talking, laughing, and pointing at some girls in the front of the line. Mya notices and feels that same threatened, annoyed feeling, but decides to stay quiet and get her breakfast, rolling her eyes to herself. One of the boys steps backwards onto her feet, crushing her new white shoes. "Watch where you're stepping!" she tells him. His friend turns around and says, "Why don't YOU watch yourself, #$%^@?!" This is the third time this morning that she has been called "that word," and it isn't even 8:00 a.m. Mya physically can't stay calm any longer.

She verbally explodes as her body's stress response system can no longer hold back the fight mode. She unloads every vulgarity she can think of onto these boys, but never throws a punch or kick, instead just lunging and yelling, unloading her pent-up verbal ammunition.

As she explodes with the anger she had contained all morning, the principal walks up to her. Mya has been called "frequent-flyer" in the principal's office this year, and the principal believes they have a "good" rapport. She lectures Mya about why she shouldn't behave the way she does. She gives Mya second chances when she shows "attitude" toward her teachers who don't like her, and she has only suspended Mya a day here and a day there when she could have suspended her for much longer.

The principal drags her away. Mya is hysterical at this point, tears streaming down her face. She is shaking and still lunging at the boys. "Come with me NOW." The boys slip away into the crowded cafeteria and seem to remain anonymous. They don't get blamed for Mya's outburst as the straw that broke the camel's back. The principal herds Mya into the office, putting her into a remote room where all the "trouble-makers" are detained until the school decides their fate.

"You need to sit there and calm yourself down! There is no room for that kind of behavior here at school!" says the principal.

"But did you hear what they called me?" sobs Mya.

"I don't care what they called you. That is no excuse for behaving the way you did! Those kinds of outbursts are unacceptable. There is no place for it here and I will not tolerate that kind of behavior from you in my school. I am suspending you for five days."

Mya's sobs are uncontrollable as she gulps for air, shaking and hyperventilating. They are sobs coming from a crack inside her soul, letting out all the pain, sorrow, and injustice that overwhelm her thirteen-year-old life. They could only be described as "soul sobs."

Through her tears Mya says, "This just feels so wrong. Everyone knows it's wrong, but they are all too afraid to do anything about it."

Trauma and Children

As a teacher and coach, I worked in schools that served students with high levels of trauma and poverty. During this time, it became very clear to me that trauma can strike all children, especially those who have experienced generational poverty, but African American students were punished at much higher rates than other students for their stress responses. These punishments (suspensions, expulsions) perpetuated the problem and retraumatized the students instead of educating and caring for them. It seems that this problem of systemic racism only creates more trauma, pain, and suffering in the lives of Black students. The traditional American school system punishes students for their trauma, which disconnects us from our humanity. This punitive system has been "business as usual" throughout our school systems and has been largely unnoticed and ignored by anyone who hasn't been directly affected by it.

This punitive system disconnects us from the human being behind the behavior. When a child exhibits a fight or flight reaction, it is most likely due to an activated stress response, and an overactive stress response is most likely due to trauma. The stress response (aka fight or flight) is the brain's natural way of protecting itself from danger. This common belief in having punishing consequences for the stress response retraumatizes our most vulnerable children and creates more fighting and fleeing, which then leads to more punishing. Traumatized children are suspended, expelled, arrested, and put into prison.

Our real job should be to teach children how to understand their brains and their stress response, and then how to self-regulate. But how can we teach them these important skills when we don't understand them ourselves?

Most adults do not understand how the brain works. We have not been taught about our stress response and have not been taught how to self-regulate. I believe that if we as a society understand the stress response and the reasons we react the ways we do under perceived threats, then we can connect and communicate with each other rather than reacting in fear, blame and punishment. My intention for this book is to shed a light on the stress response and how it is so misunderstood, especially by those who have been fortunate enough to not experience the types of extreme trauma that many children have unfortunately experienced.

Disconnection happens because we are often living from our own perspectives. I hope that this book sheds some light on the reasons we may not understand each other so that we can bridge the gaps that have been causing pain and misunderstandings.

My job at Mya's school was to teach the teachers and administrators how the brain responds to trauma. The organization where I worked was wonderful in the way that it used science to explain fight or flight responses and gave perspective on why children may "act out" in school. But even though I was able to help children and teachers understand and manage their stress responses, the program failed to create lasting change because it didn't change the policies. The policies were still bad policies designed to punish children instead of teaching them. Students were still suspended for multiple days just because of dysregulated stress responses. Mya was going to be suspended for five days because of her outburst in the cafeteria rather than creating a regulation plan for her to learn about the ways her brain reacts to stress and perceived threats. If the policies remain the same, how can the hard-working change makers make any progress?

3
MY STORY AS A NEW TEACHER

The first days, weeks, and months of the school year are often the most exhausting moments of teachers' lives, especially for new teachers, and especially in schools where there is a lot of trauma. No amount of preparation can prepare someone for the realities of those first few moments of being a teacher in a traditional school system where students experience high levels of trauma. Teachers have made it through early education and through a college education program, practicums, internships, major projects and presentations, student teaching and the numerous tests required to become licensed. Then they make it through online applications, fingerprints, job fairs, and interviews. Teachers jump through a lot of hoops to get their teaching positions. New teachers arrive excited and ready to change the world, one classroom at a time.

And then reality sinks in.

My first year was quite possibly the hardest year of my life. After taking all my coursework, completing all the clinical hours in the various schools around Chicago, and completing my student teaching, I found my first job teaching fifth grade at a Chicago Public School on the West side of Chicago. I remember celebrating on the day I was hired. Finally, all my hard work and studying had paid off.

That summer, I religiously studied Harry Wong's book, *First Days of School*, planned my routines and procedures, and made sure I was as prepared as Harry said I should be.

But nothing truly prepared me. I didn't know what I didn't know. My first three weeks were good. I rehearsed my routines and procedures and got along great with my students. But then, on the third Friday, my principal came in and yelled at me in front of the class. She said they were having too much fun and should be "working" because we had a test to pass. It was true; they were having fun. But they were also learning. It just didn't look like the traditional classroom that she wanted it to look like. She said we didn't have time for fun because we had to pass the test, and if the students didn't do well, the world would basically end and the school wouldn't get funding. And then, to make matters worse, she dropped a major bombshell on me. We had three fifth grade classes at the time and two sixth grade classes. She said that since the sixth grade tests "mattered" more, she was going to take one of the fifth grade teachers, move her up to sixth grade, and then divide her entire class of fifth grade students between me and my colleague. This bombshell was dropped on Friday afternoon, and it was going to happen Monday morning.

After that, my classroom was a chaotic, overcrowded mess. I did my best with what I knew how to do, but I never felt like I was doing good enough. I'd go in early every morning and take my work home with me in the evenings. I felt like I just needed to plan better and create more engaging lessons, or yell louder so the kids could hear me better. Nothing seemed to work. Students fought with each other and ran out of the classroom. The security guard planted himself outside my door, even though I didn't want him to. I loved my students and felt like I was failing them and failing their educations. Every day I went on with my lessons as planned, never giving up, not even on the day when a girl tried to stab a boy with a pair of scissors. Nothing in my education classes could have prepared me for this.

One day, a very friendly woman showed up. She may have been an angel. Her name was Velena Miller and she was a consultant sent to work with teachers in high trauma urban schools. None of the other teachers wanted her lurking around their classrooms. They didn't trust her and didn't want her telling them what to do. I, on the other hand, wanted all the help I could get. I was on a sinking ship and if another adult was willing to come aboard and help me save my classroom, I said thank you.

She was one of the only people that believed in me that year. I didn't believe in myself, so it was great to have one person cheering me on. Teaching can be an isolating job, and I think that many teachers struggle in isolation. I was fortunate to have her support.

My classroom was probably the worst of the worst. Kids were running around, throwing things, throwing each other, hitting each other, sleeping, leaving the classroom, shouting, talking, not listening to me, fighting, etc. They were doing everything that Harry Wong and all of my education professors said they shouldn't do. I loved them, and I was failing them. Did I mention that we didn't even have recess at this school? Without recess, the kids didn't have a proper outlet for all their energy.

About halfway through the year, my insomnia started. I would wrack my brain all day to figure out what I could do differently the next day, how I could fix this. How could I make this better? I became obsessed, but nothing worked. During this time, I desperately searched for a solution, my brain never shutting off. I couldn't give up on the possibility of a better way.

Halfway through winter break I started having back to school nightmares. I specifically remember one terrible, vivid dream. I dreamed I was back to school and I realized I hadn't gotten dressed. I had no clothes! It was embarrassing and horrible. And then in the dream I remembered that I had a spare outfit in my desk drawer. I opened the drawer and the extra outfit inside was a bright orange prison jumpsuit.

My subconscious was telling me something I already knew. I was imprisoned by my new career. It was such a vulnerable feeling, to be responsible for the lives, safety, and education of 35+ students who knew I had no idea how to teach them.

Now, after twelve years of public school teaching and several more years of coaching and training in the topic of trauma informed care, I understand more of what was happening in the brains and souls of my students and myself.

I survived my first year (barely). I used up all my sick days plus a couple of extra days because I got really sick. The stress and insomnia took a toll on my body and my mind. I had a cold that was so severe I had to stay in bed for two entire weeks per doctor's orders. During that time, my students were left with unequipped substitute teachers, which created even more chaos and tragedy. When I came back, the school had suspended all of my most vulnerable students, who were sent home (out to the streets) to fend for themselves all day while their guardians were working. That devastated me because I knew that as bad as my classroom environment was, at least they knew I loved them, and they weren't outside being hurt.

I'm telling you my first-year teaching experience because I think it is more common than the general population realizes. It is difficult to find out that you are not equipped for the profession you have spent years training for. Teachers who work in traditional schools are often living in a survival zone. It is unbelievably hard when we are only trained in the academic and teaching parts, and not in the trauma and relationship building parts, which is the missing piece of the puzzle. Most people who haven't gone through that time of survival mode don't understand the toll it takes on the body and brain. Living in the stress response (fight, flight, freeze mode) for long periods of time can cause PTSD. This is true for teachers, and it is especially true for our students, who often have high-level trauma that they are dealing with daily. This is why supporting teachers is vital for our society. Our students, especially our must vulnerable, stressed, high trauma students, need teachers who understand the effects of trauma and stress.

4
THE EFFECTS OF STRESS AND TRAUMA

We All Have a Stress Response

Our brains are uniquely equipped to keep us safe. Our primitive brains evolved to be on alert for any real or perceived danger that could threaten our survival. The sound of an unfamiliar noise could have meant a bear or lion rustling in the nearby leaves. We had to be prepared to either fight, run away, or freeze and hide. Our fight or flight response is nature's way of always keeping us subtly alert to potential dangers or threats around us.

While we no longer have everyday threats of large animal predators, our modern threats such as road rage, arguments, nasty emails, or being low on money for bills illicit the same response: **Fight, Flight or Freeze**.

The fight, flight, or freeze reaction is actually a hormonal response. Sensing danger or threats, our brains respond by pumping adrenaline and cortisol into our bloodstream to power us with the explosive energy we need to fight or run away.

Stress can be good if it's in small doses that are well managed. This kind of stress promotes growth and learning. However, if stress is constant, unpredictable, and unmanaged, it can create lasting changes in the brain and body, causing health problems, inflammation, and hypersensitivity to smaller doses of stress like a shortened fuse. This can lead to feelings of anxiousness, loss of control, fatigue, drained emotional and physical energy, and burnout.

The Difference Between Stress and Trauma

Stress and trauma are different variations of the same thing, and shame has similar feelings as the stress response.

Stress is a state of mental and emotional strain or tension that results from adverse or demanding circumstances. Stress is anything that challenges our system. Stress can be positive, and we need some stress to grow and adapt and change. People learn when they challenge their systems in a controlled way. Muscles grow when we apply some controlled stress. Everyday stress, when managed, is not necessarily a bad thing. It can promote growth when the doses are small, predictable, and well-managed, and when we have the necessary supports in place to help us cope with stress. This is how we build resilience and growth.

Examples of ways managed stress can promote growth:

- Learning unfamiliar concepts and studying to pass a test creates new neural pathways and growth.
- Lifting weights stresses the muscles in a way to grow stronger.

Trauma or traumatic stress is any event or a series of events that are so stressful that they leave us feeling overwhelmed, unsafe, or helpless. We feel out of control. We feel powerless. Trauma is the most intense form of stress that we can experience. Trauma activates our survival brain and makes us go into survival mode. When we experience trauma, our brain's primary goal is to keep us alive.

Examples of trauma:

- Childhood neglect or abuse
- Violence
- Racism
- Homelessness

Shame is a painful feeling of stressful self-hatred and comes from the belief that we are flawed, inadequate, not good enough, or lesser than others. Shame can be caused by trauma.

Trauma and stress are not "one size fits all." What may feel stressful for one person may feel traumatic for another. Stress affects people very differently. Our nervous systems respond very differently. This difference in response varies from person to person depending on many factors including our individual, varying resilience to stress.

A person's ability to self-regulate or to be resilient when under stress and pressure depends a lot on the connections and relationships we have in our lives. Shame also plays a role in our ability to self-regulate. If we felt responsible for certain traumas during our developmental years, this trauma could turn into shame and be carried with us throughout a lifetime. It has an impact on how helpless we feel or how empowered and resilient we can become.

A lot of this depends on our early life experiences when our brains were developing. Did we have a lot of stress or trauma in childhood? Did we have strong connections, relationships or resilience builders during those formative years? Or were we more vulnerable to feeling helpless? Did we feel we had to survive on our own?

Stress affects people on a spectrum, depending on:

1. Early traumas or shame and/or our positive connective experiences. From the perspective of brain science, this would be how our brains developed the neural pathways and associations, as well as attachments with our caregivers.

2. Resilience factors that can include positive relationships and connections with the people who love us, and from the spiritual viewpoint, our connection with a higher power, our inner wisdom, intuition, or anything you may call God.

3. Our ability to self-regulate.

In my years of teaching and trauma-informed coaching in schools, I have seen and heard my share of trauma stories from students and colleagues. Children experience some things that many teachers have never had to fathom, and when they find out some of the more extreme stories, they often say that if they had known, they would have understood the student's behavior. It is my stance that we just assume all students who struggle with "behavior" have experienced some form of trauma in their lives. Here are a few stories about common scenarios that children go through.

Anthony

Anthony was a student who was being raised by his grandmother, who worked twelve-hour days in order to take care of him. His mother was murdered when he was two years old, and his father was serving a lifetime prison sentence. Anthony would often cry in class and shutdown randomly during the school day, putting his head on his desk. He was a talented artist and could illustrate the scenes of the stories that the teacher read aloud with amazing detail. His teacher was looking into art camps for him for the summertime because she didn't want him to spend his days alone while his grandmother worked such long hours. Unfortunately, the classroom had a substitute teacher one day when his regular teacher was sick. The substitute did not have a relationship with Anthony and sent him to the office for punishment. The school suspended Anthony for ten days on a day in May, preventing him from returning to school at all.

Trish

Patricia was an elementary student who had been adopted by a family who had many foster children. She and her biological brother had witnessed the murder/suicide of their biological parents, which was a horrific and unfathomable trauma for the children. Their new adoptive parents were abusive to Patricia, putting her on unreasonable diets and making her run laps in the yard. Patricia was desperate for a loving connection and would take trinkets and toys from home to give to her teachers at school. Her adoptive parents accused her of stealing and branded her a "thief." They refused to allow her to carry a backpack to and from school because they said they could not trust her. One day the principal of the school sent Patricia home with a brand-new backpack full of markers, crayons and supplies. Her adoptive mother came to the school to return it and complain, explaining that Patricia was a thief and was not allowed to have such nice things.

Patricia's adoptive parents gave her the nickname, "Patty," but she did not like this name. Her teacher playfully suggested the nickname "Trish" as an alternative to Patty. Patricia was delighted by it and began writing it at the top of all her school papers.

One day, Patricia's mother came in to say that she was not going to allow her to be called "Trish" and she was forbidding Patricia, her classmates, and the teacher from using the playful nickname.

In school, Patricia was a wonderful, kind, caring student, and friend to her classmates. She thrived in her safe learning environment. However, the adoptive family decided that they no longer wanted her and relinquished her back to the state. Many years later, the teacher was told that Patricia was adopted by a wonderful family and officially changed her name to Trish.

Geoffrey

Geoffrey was a student who made up unbelievable tales of adventure. His clothes were always unwashed, and when he arrived at school on Mondays, he would tell his teacher stories of weekend trips to amusement parks, lobster dinners, and short weekend vacations at the beach. Many students believed him, but others accused him of lying. Some of his teachers punished him for not telling the truth by sentencing him to detention. He always appeared cheerful and helpful, doing his best to be an excellent student. The only time he cried was when his teacher saw a bedbug crawling up his neck from under his shirt. She quietly asked him to hold still as she ran and got a Ziplock bag to capture it with. Geoffrey stood as still as a statue, tears rolling down his brave face. A few years later, his father was arrested for trafficking children, and Geoffrey was sent to live with a foster family.

These are just a few stories that are much more common than most of us realize. When we recognize how common trauma is, we can begin to understand that all students may have experienced it. If we create our learning spaces around this assumption, students can feel safe when they are at school. School may not remove the trauma, but it can give students a break from it rather than punishing or retraumatizing them for their reactions.

When we understand the impact of trauma on physical, emotion and mental health, and the implications on behavioral issues, we can acknowledge students rather than punish them. When there is a behavior problem, there is usually, if not always, trauma at the root of it. Ask, "What happened to this person to cause this behavior?" rather than assuming the student is "bad." You don't have to know what the trauma is. Just assume that if there is a behavior issue, there has been a trauma experience.

When we understand trauma, we can then understand how schools can retraumatize with punitive systems.

<u>Sienna</u>

Sienna was a middle school student who had experienced domestic violence in her home. Her teacher, who was an overly controlling man with many biases towards his students, often raised his voice at Sienna. One day, Sienna felt like her teacher was trying to pick a fight with her. She experienced a fight or flight reaction and ran out of the classroom to try to escape the situation. The teacher called the office and the office sent several security officers, equipped with walkie-talkies to "capture" Sienna. Eventually, Sienna was suspended for leaving her classroom.

Schools can be terrifying places for students who have experienced trauma, especially when there is a perceived power differential with controlling, punitive systems. When teacher stress is epidemic, students may feel they are not liked or take it personally.

Understanding trauma and the brain can promote a culture of safety and empowerment, and increase learning. When we understand trauma and the stress response and when all staff, teachers, and students are educated on self-regulation skills, schools can be calmer, safer environments for everyone involved.

Reflection

What did you know about the prevalence and effects of childhood trauma before reading this book?

_____
_____
_____
_____
_____

What do you know about your students' trauma experiences?

_____
_____
_____
_____
_____

How do you think trauma has impacted your students' experience in school?

_____
_____
_____
_____
_____

The Definitions of Dysregulated vs. Self-Regulated

Before we continue, let's define some terms that will help better clarify the stress response and how to manage it.

Dysregulated:

When we say someone is dysregulated, it means they are showing signs of the stress response. This means that something has activated their survival brain and they are disconnected from their sense of self. When a person is dysregulated, they do not have access to the rational, reasoning part of their brain and will have trouble thinking and using their intuition.

When a person becomes dysregulated, they may show it in a number of ways:

- Agitation or anxiousness
- Hyper vigilance and being on the lookout for threats
- Disassociation or being shut down
- Aggressiveness or Defensiveness
- Taking things very personally as a threat
- Loss of self-control
- Inability to think clearly, inability to concentrate, foggy headedness

Showing signs of being dysregulated means the person is showing signs that their stress response has been activated and their survival brain is kicking in to help them fight, run away, or freeze. For a person to be considered dysregulated, they don't have to be in the full-blown fight, flight or freeze of the stress response. Being dysregulated can simply mean that the survival part of their brain has picked up on something and is on alert for potential threats in their environment. Shame can also make a person show similar symptoms.

Self-Regulated:

When someone is regulated, or "self-regulated," they are connected to their sense of self and have full access to the rational, logical, "thinking" part of their brain. When a person is self-regulated:

- They can think and communicate clearly and rationally
- They are in control of their body
- They are in control of their emotional responses
- Their body feels calm and safe
- They feel emotionally safe
- They feel connected to their inner wisdom/intuition

This awareness is a crucial first step in understanding the stress and trauma response. When we start to see or feel ourselves getting agitated, we know that it is a natural response, and everyone experiences it to some degree or another.

Shame can add further stress on top of a stress response when people do not understand their brain's stress response system. This occurs because oftentimes, when a person feels out of control or dysregulated, they think there is something wrong with them.

Reflection questions:

1. Have you ever noticed yourself feeling dysregulated? What were the signs?

_____

_____

_____

_____

_____

2. How do you feel when you become dysregulated? Do you feel like fighting? Running away? Shutting down? Or some combination of the three?

_____

_____

_____

_____

Describe how you feel when you become dysregulated:

_____

_____

_____

_____

The Adverse Childhood Experiences Study

Trauma Informed Care is based on the Adverse Childhood Experiences Study. Because of the study, we know how prevalent childhood trauma is in society and how it affects the lives of those who experience it in the long term.

The Adverse Childhood Experiences Study, or "ACE" study, was based on research by Kaiser Permanente and the CDC between 1995 and 1997. The study seems to show a correlation between adverse childhood experiences and negative health and social outcomes throughout the lifetime of participants.

The study began when Vincent Felitti, head of Kaiser Permanente's Department of Preventative Medicine in San Diego, interviewed people who had left the obesity clinic program. Dr. Felitti discovered that a high number of the people he interviewed had experienced abuse or neglect in childhood and wondered if there might have been a correlation between trauma and the obesity they were experiencing.

Dr. Felitti joined forces with Robert Anda from the Centers for Disease Control and Prevention (CDC) and they surveyed over 17,000 Kaiser Permanente patient volunteers, asking ten questions about childhood abuse and neglect. For each question, a "yes" answer to a trauma would give one point on the ACE score.

Felitti and Anda's study seemed to show that adverse childhood experiences are common and there seems to be a correlation between adverse childhood experiences (trauma) and health problems or social problems into adulthood, including:

- Asthma
- Arthritis
- Cancer
- Diabetes
- Heart attacks, heart disease, strokes
- Vision problems

There was also an increased correlation in smoking, alcoholism, drug abuse and suicide attempts in participants with an increased ACE score.

This is important because it shows that trauma and stressful events have an impact on our brain, body and nervous systems. Trauma in childhood can change the way our brains develop, change the way we react to stress and future traumas, and can have long term negative heath impacts.

From a scientific point of view, it is said that the constant release of stress hormones (adrenaline and cortisol) "short circuit" the body's system, which kind of "fray the wires." If a person is always on alert or dysregulated, they are going to feel anxious and stressed out all the time and their bodies will feel the nervous effects of the stress hormones designed to make them fight or run fast. They will have a hard time feeling a sense of safety when the body and brain don't get a break from the stress hormones.

It seems that trauma can cause our brains to develop in ways that have lifelong negative impacts to our physical and emotional health and change the way we relate to others in personal and professional relationships.

From the spiritual perspective, these traumas create pain and shame that create a heaviness that the soul must carry throughout life until the person can process it and put it down.

Trauma Informed Care

Because of the strong correlation between ACE scores and negative health outcomes, many organizations have adopted "trauma informed" approaches. Schools, hospitals, and prisons are hotbeds for the effects of trauma. Children bring their trauma to schools and then get punished for it. This constant punishment puts them on the path to prison. In hospitals, healthcare professionals encounter dysregulated patients who react with violence when they are afraid.

In workplace environments, employees and leaders bring their traumas to work along with the shame of thinking there must be something wrong with them. Trauma, shame, and stress are common unspoken ingredients that can cloud our interactions and communications. Every time we have a stressful interaction, it is likely that an activated stress response is an underlying factor for the misunderstanding and miscommunication. Humans carry their trauma with them and some of our reactions under stress are the reactions of our survival brain, not purposeful malicious acts. Many institutions are becoming "trauma informed." According to the National Center for Trauma Informed Care, being trauma informed means:

1. Recognizing the widespread impact of trauma
2. Recognizing traumatic symptoms (signs and behaviors of dysregulation/stress response)
3. Responding effectively
4. Actively preventing re-traumatization.

5
THE BRAIN

In this chapter, we'll go through the main parts of the brain, when they develop, and their functions. When you can better understand the brain, you can better understand the stress response.

The Brainstem

The brainstem develops in utero. Its primary purpose is to regulate our survival functions such as heart rate, blood pressure, body temperature, and glucose levels. The brainstem keeps us alive. It is our survival brain and is not responsible for logic, thinking, reasoning, or making decisions. Instead, it is reactive. Its job is to react to anything that may pose a threat to our survival.

The brainstem helps us react to threats by causing us to do things like quickly jumping out of the way of a speeding car, ducking when a big rock hits the windshield, or getting startled when we hear a loud noise. If you were to touch something hot, the brainstem helps you jerk your hand away before you can think about it. It keeps you safe and alive.

The brainstem acts as a filtering system for all the information that comes in through our senses. All information is filtered through the brainstem including sounds, smells, sights, the amount of oxygen you need, and whether you feel hungry or thirsty.

The filter asks:

"Is this familiar and safe?"-

"Is this familiar and associated with a past threat and therefore unsafe?"

"Is this unfamiliar and therefore unsafe?"

If it all feels familiar and safe, the information is then allowed to continue up from the brainstem toward the cortex.

If information is flagged as unsafe, the brainstem stops information from going up, preventing it from getting to the "thinking" part of the brain and rerouting it toward a bodily reaction such as running, ducking, or jumping. Let's say you're driving along thinking about what groceries you need. A car almost hits you, causing you to become startled. You react by swerving and doing what you need to do to escape the danger, and momentarily you lose all concentration of what you were thinking about before the near accident.

A Note About Uncertainty

Uncertainty can be very stressful for the brain because it is flagged as a potential threat. Long periods of uncertainty can put the brain into a constant state of alarm, especially over long periods of time. You've probably noticed this during the uncertainty of the coronavirus pandemic. In children, the uncertainty and dysregulation caused by something like a pandemic may show up as tantrums or "misbehavior."

The Limbic System and Amygdala

The limbic system develops during adolescent years and is responsible for mediating behavior and regulating emotions, motivation, memory, and relationships with others. For the sake of this book, we can call the limbic system our emotional brain or "teenage" brain. The limbic system operates with the endocrine or hormonal system and the autonomic nervous system. For our purposes, we are going to highlight our focus on the amygdala, which is a part of the limbic system.

Just as toddlers learn to walk by practicing, falling and getting back up over and over, adolescents learn to relate to each other by practicing. As the limbic system develops in the teen years, adolescents learn how to relate to each other similar to the way toddlers learn how to walk when their diencephalon, the part of the brain responsible for muscle movement, is developing. The limbic system is responsible for our relationships.

The amygdala is considered to be the deepest and most primitive part of the limbic system. It records memories and emotions such as fear, anger, and sadness. The amygdala stores the memories of events and emotions so that the individual may quickly recognize them in the future.

When we are traumatized, associations with our trauma will be stored in our amygdala and when we encounter those associations or triggers even years later, it will cause our amygdala to fire up to alert us of possible danger. You can see how this could mean that negative associations and emotional memories could be stored in this emotional part of the brain, and trauma will certainly get stored here.

The Cortex and Mirror Neurons

The Cortex

The cortex develops throughout childhood and adolescence and is not fully developed until a person reaches their mid-20s. The cortex is the most complex part of the brain and is responsible for logic, creativity, attention, memory perception, awareness, consciousness, and problem solving. It is the "thinking part" of our brain. The cortex is also our executive functioning part of the brain. The cortex is required for our voluntary activities, planning and organization.

We must have full access to the cortex to think clearly and with reason. Remember, information comes in through the brainstem and travels up through the limbic system and then reaches the cortex. If the information gets stuck at the brainstem or the limbic system, it is unable to reach the cortex, or "reasoning" part of the brain.

Part of Brain	When it develops	Functions
Brainstem "Survival Brain"	In Utero	Basic Survival: heartbeat, breathing, glucose levels
Diencephalon/ Midbrain "Motor Brain"	Toddler years	Movement/Motor functions
Limbic System & Amygdala "Emotional Brain"	Adolescence	Emotions/ emotional regulation Relationships
Cortex "Thinking Brain"	Not fully developed until age 25+. Continues to develop throughout life as learning takes place	Logical reasoning, long term planning, thinking, executive functioning, rationalizing

Mirror Neurons

Our brains are designed to quickly scan and pick up the emotions and behaviors of others. Mirror neurons, which are found in the cortex and have been observed in other primate species, may be important for understanding the actions and intentions of others. They may be the neural basis for our emotional capacity and empathy.

Mirror neurons allow us to learn through imitation, reflecting body language, facial expressions, and emotions.

Mirror neurons are believed to help us subconsciously imitate the emotions and behaviors of others. They are said to be what causes babies to imitate their caregivers, and they are said to be responsible for making us fall in love.

From the spiritual perspective, I like to explain this as picking up the energy from those around us. It is what gives us the ability to read a room and feel the heaviness of tension after an argument or the lightness in a room of happy people.

Recap of Key Points

1. The brainstem is our survival brain and is responsible for keeping us alive. It develops in utero.

2. The limbic system/amygdala is our "emotional brain" and is responsible for regulating emotions and storing emotional memories. It develops during our teenage years.

3. The cortex is our "thinking brain" and is where logic, reasoning, planning, and executive functioning take place.

4. Information travels up from the brainstem to reach the cortex. Information must successfully pass through the filtering system of the brainstem to reach the cortex. If it does not pass through the filtering system, a person will become dysregulated and not have full access to their cortex. They will not be able to reason or think clearly.

5. Mirror neurons are thought to allow humans to feel empathy and mirror the emotions and behaviors of others. They may also be responsible for all that we can sense at a subconscious level.

6
HOW THE STRESS RESPONSE WORKS

Now that we have a simplified view of the brain and its functions, we are going to talk about how the stress response works. Understanding how and why the stress response works is the key to:

- Recognizing when your stress response gets activated or triggered.
- Recognizing the triggers.
- Recognizing the stress response in the people you are communicating with as a natural survival response as opposed to disrespectful, voluntary, personal attacks on you, your character, or your professionalism.

We are going to talk more about the "survival brain" and what happens when the stress response gets activated, as well as a more in depth look at how stress and energy can be contagious when our mirror neurons sense danger. In this chapter, we are going to look at the Stress Response in our modern life and the way it shows up in everyday situations. We will discuss ways we can recognize it in ourselves and others so we can stay regulated and reduce the stress contagion.

Survival Brain

No one is "immune" to stress. All brains experience stress and stress is a necessary ingredient for learning and growth to occur. When stress is controlled and predictable, we can become more resilient and experience growth.

Stress becomes a problem when it is unpredictable, severe and chronic. This is when stress becomes trauma, and we can become vulnerable to the negative effects of stress if it is left unchecked.

As we talked about in Chapter 3, the brainstem is the part of the brain responsible for keeping us alive. It controls our heartbeat, breathing, and other survival functions. Information travels from the bottom up, flowing through the brainstem and up towards the cortex. The brainstem is responsible for all our survival functions.

The brainstem acts as a filter for all information and stimuli coming in, and this information must pass through the brainstem's filter in order to continue traveling up to the cortex, which is the "thinking" part of the brain. This filter in the brainstem is on the lookout for anything that may be a potential threat to survival. The limbic system & amygdala is the emotional part of the brain, which is also part of our lower brain. For the purposes of this explanation of the stress response, I am going to refer to these parts of the brain as our "survival brain."

If the information coming in is familiar and safe, it is permitted to continue traveling up towards the logical, rational thinking brain. However, if this information is unfamiliar, or associated with a past threat (trauma), the survival brain's "filtering system" flags it as potentially UNSAFE.

This means that when information is predictable in a neutral or positive way, it is filtered as safe. When the filter catches something unpredictable, it is flagged as a potential threat to our survival, because we have nothing to match it up with yet, and it gets "paused." (This is why uncertainty and unpredictability can be so stressful. The survival brain does not feel comfortable with the unknown, but learning and growth can take place when we lean into the unknown and take managed risks). When the filter catches something associated with a past threat (trauma), the information is classified as unsafe and information is not permitted to continue up toward the cortex.

When information is filtered as familiar, it is safe. This is why predictability keeps us calm, and we are able to reason and think clearly in that calm state. When the survival brain filters information as safe and familiar, the information continues traveling up towards the cortex. We remain calm or alert and we have full access to our cortex. Small doses of stress or new stimuli create new neural pathways if we can control some levels of predictability.

When information is flagged as unfamiliar, unsafe, or associated with past trauma, it is labeled on a spectrum from potentially unsafe all the way to danger. This is when we become dysregulated or "in the stress response." The information gets stopped by the filtering system and is prevented from traveling up to the cortex. We do not have full access to our cortex when we are dysregulated or in the stress response. People get in arguments because they are actually "out of their minds."

This is why we can get triggered with "emotional threats" as well as physical threats. Remember, the limbic system and amygdala are responsible for emotional response and storing emotional memories, so all threats to our physical and emotional survival are flagged by our survival brains.

If incoming information is perceived as a threat, (real, perceived, or related to a past emotional or physical threat or trauma), the stress response is activated and the "survival brain" stops allowing access to the cortex because surviving is first and foremost; it is more important than thinking or calm reasoning when presented with a possible threat. The survival brain is doing its job; it has perceived a threat to our survival, so it prepares to do what it needs to keep us alive.

Recap of Key Points

- The Brainstem and Limbic System (Amygdala) are the lower parts of our brain responsible for survival and emotional safety. We call this the "survival brain."

- The survival brain is always filtering information as safe or unsafe. Information is either safe and predictable or unsafe, unpredictable, or related to past threat.

- When a threat is detected, the survival brain prepares to respond to the threat, and the STRESS RESPONSE is ACTIVATED.

The Activated Stress Response

The lower parts of the brain can be considered our survival brain and are responsible for keeping us alive and safe. When our survival brain detects a potential threat, the stress response is activated.

Keep in mind, if the brain is activated "lightly" by something that is unpredictable and the survival brain doesn't have enough information to know the level of threat, we can become dysregulated. This is where there can be a spectrum of dysregulation. In a school setting, this would look like kids not being able to sit still or focus. They may not be fighting or fleeing, but they are definitely fidgeting and not paying attention to their lessons.

Within a split second of perceiving the threat, the fight or flight response is activated, and the brain's top priority is to keep us alive and survive the danger. Access to the cortex (thinking brain) is cut off because the body and brain need to conserve energy that would be used for executive functions like thinking, planning, and reasoning so it can get us out of danger as soon as possible. **This means when the stress response is activated, we do not have full access to the thinking part of our brain. We are unable to think clearly.**

When the survival brain detects a threat, it makes the "emergency" decision to engage the fight or flight response. The cortex will not be "online," therefore it is not involved in the process. The cortex cannot overrule the survival brain in this brief split second.

Stress hormones are released, including adrenaline and cortisol, to prepare the body to escape this danger by fighting, fleeing, or freezing. These hormones increase the heart rate and elevate the blood pressure while redirecting energy that would be supplied to the cortex for thinking and decision making to fight the threat, or to power the body into running away to escape the danger. Some people freeze, and the body dissociates or shuts down. When this happens, the person disconnects from themselves as well as the current threat or situation. The freeze response is common but is less noticeable in society. We see fighting a lot, or fleeing, but those who dissociate tend to fly under the radar. Oftentimes when students dissociate, teachers might think they are just trying to sleep. During dissociation, the person may feel disconnected from their surroundings completely.

A person who experiences stress can also start to become dysregulated without having a full-blown fight or flight response. Dysregulation often starts with some agitation, irrational thoughts, sweating, or emotional reactivity. A dysregulated person is not able to think at full capacity, and dysregulation can range from being on high alert, to fight/flight/freeze, or even losing consciousness all together.

The stress response varies from person to person, often depending upon:

- the amount of trauma or stress in their background
- their ability to recognize the signs of their own dysregulation early enough to self-regulate
- the connections and relationships to calm, regulated people in their surroundings.

Depending on many individual factors including the ability and awareness to self-regulate, a person can notice the signs of dysregulation in themselves early enough to self-regulate and avoid going into full-blown fight or flight mode. When a person understands their brain, triggers, and personal feelings associated with dysregulation, they can recognize what is happening, remove themselves from the perceived threat, and use their own individualized self-regulation techniques to calm down and regain full access to their cortex.

However, when someone is in an extremely vulnerable state, they may feel helpless. This dysregulated state of helplessness can escalate quickly into the full-blown stress response of fight or flight. This is when many regrettable fights, arguments or actions happen.

It is for this reason that people in unpredictable or fearful situations may feel especially helpless. The fact that we all have varying degrees of past trauma combined with uncertain or scary situations may make some of us more reactive than others. People who have had a lot of traumas can become hypervigilant and hyper-reactive. They may be always on high alert or react more explosively to smaller perceived threats.

Escalations happen with people who have had a lot of trauma or stress in their lives. This is because others try to reason with them or calm them down, which only makes them more dysregulated. Remember, a person cannot reason when they are dysregulated, and it may be perceived as an attack, furthering their escalation. Another reason escalation happens with people who have experienced a lot of trauma is that they may already be hypervigilant or hyper-reactive, which will make them overreact to perceived threats that may not be real dangers. Also note that stress is contagious due to mirror neurons. Dysregulated people can affect others around them to become dysregulated as well.

Now that we have discussed the stress response and know why it happens, lets look at some ways stress can be contagious.

Stress is Contagious: More About Mirror Neurons

As we discussed in Chapter 3 when learning about the parts and function of the brain, it is believed that mirror neurons are responsible for understanding and mimicking the emotions in others, and they may play a role in "emotional contagion."

Babies with loving caregivers develop a healthy sense of self through "mirroring." Their emotions are mirrored back to them by their caregivers and the people who love them. When the baby or child is loved, the loving adult mirrors love back to them and they feel safe, secure and lovable.

This can work in the opposite way too. If a baby or child has a caregiver that is not as caring or loving, the baby will get unloving reflections mirrored back to them.

These mirror neurons are partly responsible for the way we perceive others' opinions or feelings about us. We feel like we can read their feelings about us as they are mirrored back to us.

All relationships, interactions, places, environments, or situations have their own particular energy or mood. It can feel heavy, light, calm, tense, scary, chaotic, orderly, warm, or cold depending on a multitude of factors. This energy can shift and is usually felt or perceived by those in the situation, environment or relationship on a conscious or subconscious level.

If someone is dysregulated, their energy can shift the energy in the environment. The others in the environment will sense or perceive this dysregulated energy, which can be perceived as a threat to their survival brains and activate their stress response.

The stress response is "contagious" because our brains are designed to scan and pick up the emotions of others. When someone is in a dysregulated and agitated state, our survival brains are going to pick up on the angry, argumentative, potentially violent energy and interpret it as a threat. This activates our stress response and then like a ping-pong ball, the other person's mirror neurons will perceive our heightened stress response or dysregulation. This ping-ponging back and forth can escalate until we have a full-blown storm of stress response. This is how a regulated person ends up in arguments, fights, disagreements, and with hurt feelings when communicating with someone who is dysregulated.

Stress contagion is why schools, hospitals, prisons and workplaces can become toxic with stress. Everyone's fear and dysregulation mixes together, creating a cyclone of toxicity. It's unhealthy for our minds and bodies. It's important, when talking about this, not to blame the dysregulated person.

Educators and Healthcare Professionals can be especially vulnerable to "compassion fatigue" as they take care of others who are in stressful, traumatic situations. The constant exposure to the stress and trauma responses of others can often physically and emotionally exhaust those who are in the caretaker role. For this reason, it is important to develop self-regulation and self-care routines for those who are in these important roles.

What the Stress Response Looks Like in Modern Life

Our primitive brains developed to protect us from danger, but in recent times, the dangers have changed more than our brain's survival response. The threats that we used to face involved large, predatory creatures that are less often encountered in this modern era. Now our threats may be more sophisticated and less likely to be a physical danger. But that doesn't make them less threatening to our survival brains. Some of our modern threats include:

- job loss/financial loss
- loss of social or professional image
- embarrassment
- driving in heavy traffic
- arguing with a friend, partner or colleague
- pandemics
- isolation
- threats of scarcity
- unpredictability or uncertainty
- anything related to past threats (trauma)
- anything that threatens our modern survival

Common Scenarios of Stress Response and Emotional Contagion

In a Dating Relationship

Scenario: Jennifer's new boyfriend Phil sends her a text message that she doesn't quite understand. Something in the message behind his words puts her on alert. She decides to call him to clarify any misunderstandings. He answers the phone begrudgingly, and says he had a terrible, stressful day at work and is now struggling to get his five-year old son into the bathtub. His son is not cooperating and is "throwing a temper tantrum." Jennifer's boyfriend is a widower and a single parent to his son. He has a high stress, high stakes job that involves high levels of unpredictability on a daily basis.

Jennifer has had a past of "disappointing" boyfriends and is always on the lookout for any behaviors that might indicate a potential "jerk." She decided to call him to clear up the situation right away. She has always operated under the belief that it's best to clear up problems right when they are happening, as soon as possible.

Jennifer didn't like Phil's tone, so she decided to "jokingly jab" him with her own sarcastic comments and said, "Wow, you sure know how to make a lady feel great. You're so romantic." Phil didn't really want to talk and had to deal with his splashing, tantrum-throwing son in the bathtub. Jennifer hung up the phone and told herself, "Wow, Phil sure has some cracks in his veneer tonight. I knew it wouldn't be long until his perfect top layer started to crumble."

What's happening here?

- Phil was dysregulated. He was experiencing the stress response from his day at work, and then from his interaction with his dysregulated son. Their interaction alone was a dysregulation cyclone, and then Jennifer's call added to it.

- Jennifer was dysregulated by the text message and potential "meaning behind the meaning." She was on high alert because of past threats, therefore was on the lookout for any dangers.

- Jennifer theoretically wanted to have a logical, reasoning, conversation. The problem was she was dysregulated, and Phil was dysregulated, so neither of them had access to their cortex. Reasoning was not possible at this time, but her stress response wanted to "clear up any threats" right away.

When one person is dysregulated, this type of stressful energy is contagious because our mirror neurons pick up on the other person's stress response. We then become dysregulated. It is impossible to reason during the stress response because nobody really has access to their cortex.

Trying to reason during a heated argument (even if it's on the phone) will likely result in escalation of the problem. ***You cannot reason with a dysregulated person.***

As you can see, not understanding the stress response can create more conflict and misunderstandings in perfectly good relationships because we tend to take being dysregulated personally or as a sign of disrespect. Often, though, it is just the brain doing its job and trying to protect us from danger.

In a Medical Setting: Patient/Healthcare Professional Escalation

A patient and their family member arrive at the emergency room with a severe medical situation. They have reasons to be dysregulated, including:

- Physical survival is being threatened by illness (Physical threat)
- Unfamiliar surroundings + Unfamiliar people (Unpredictability)

A healthcare professional arrives to care for the patient. The healthcare professional has reasons to be dysregulated, including:

- Lack of sleep due to demanding shift schedules and insomnia from stress. This lack of sleep is dysregulating in itself as sleep is a necessity for survival. This creates a more sensitized stress response and the healthcare professional is already a bit dysregulated.
- A new patient (unpredictability)
- The high stress demands of the job. Also, the last patient was angry, dysregulated, and afraid.

The healthcare professional enters the space with the new patient and their family member. The family member is already on alert and in protective mode and picks up on the dysregulation of the healthcare professional. The (dysregulated) family member begins to interrogate the healthcare professional, which the healthcare professional takes as an insult (threat) and responds in a defensive way.

- The family member insults the healthcare professional. The healthcare professional feels threated (physically, professionally, personally) and becomes even more dysregulated.

- This dysregulates the (ill) patient even more, and they feel their safety is threatened because they now think the healthcare professional doesn't care about them, and their physical survival is dependent on this healthcare professional.

This "ping-ponging" back and forth is how situations escalate, and in medical situations, hurt feelings are not the only thing at stake. Keep in mind, dysregulated people do not have full access to their cortex, therefore:

- There is a higher likelihood of medical mistakes or errors

- There is a higher likelihood of unprofessional conduct, which can result in loss of professional security

- The healthcare professional is actually at risk physically, as violence against healthcare professionals is a serious and common problem

- The healthcare professional can "carry" the stress to their next patient and the contagion continues

- The healthcare professional feels unappreciated, or even hated, devalued, and even more stressed because they have been sacrificing their health and "running on empty" yet are treated badly.

- The healthcare professional is constantly dysregulated, which floods their body with stress hormones, causing a multitude of health problems including insomnia, which will continue the dysregulation cycle.

- The healthcare professional will bring this stress and dysregulation home with them to their friends, partner and family.

- The healthcare professional may suffer from burnout and overall dissatisfaction with their life.

- They may abuse drugs, alcohol, or food to manage stress in unhealthy ways.

Common Scenario in a School

The student may experience trauma and toxic stress and bring it to school with them. School may feel unpredictable, which would make it feel unsafe simply because our brains respond to unpredictability as a threat. Ironically, students who experience high trauma may find the "safety" of school to be threatening because it is unpredictable and not like anything they have experienced before. This is common in my experience, especially in the first few weeks of school until they relax into the predictability and can trust the unfamiliar people.

Next, we have a teacher. The teacher may bring their own stress or trauma to school or may be unprepared. Teaching in itself is unpredictable and stressful, so the job itself can be dysregulating even in the most ideal scenario. Some common ways that dysregulation can spiral between teachers and students are illustrated as follows:

The teacher picks up on the child's dysregulated state noticing their behavior problems and takes it as a threat. The teacher is on high alert for this child.

The student feels this reaction from the teacher and senses the teacher is not safe or doesn't like the child. This dysregulates the child further.

The teacher picks up on this further dysregulation and feels the need to control the student, so they do something punitive or harsh, which creates a fight or flight reaction in the student.

Now the other students are feeling all this dysregulation from their classmate as well as their teacher, and they start to become dysregulated.

The teacher's mirror neurons pick up on the dysregulation in the classroom and becomes more dysregulated. The teacher tries harsher tactics to try and regain control but may come across as aggressive or threatening to the students. At this point, the teacher has lost access to their cortex and cannot rationalize. The students have lost access to their cortexes and cannot make rational choices, let alone learn.

This is an extremely common scenario in schools. Teachers have one of the most demanding and stressful jobs in our society, and they are at serious risk for burnout and health problems.

Children who have higher levels of trauma tend to suffer doubly because they get labeled as "behavior problems," and suffer re-traumatization by getting thrown out or suspended. Students that have high levels of trauma suffer at school, get suspended, and then have a much higher chance of going to prison. If you were to survey the prison population, you would find that trauma and the activation of the stress response was the root cause of it all. I think that if more people understood this, our world would be a better place.

Common Scenario in a Work Environment

Let's start with the leader. This "work environment" could be any type of business, company, institution, or place where we have a leader or leaders and employees. For the purposes of this scenario, let's call the leader the "boss."

The boss has unpredictable expectations for the employees. This unpredictability comes across as lack of communication. The employees want to do a good job, but they feel like they have to do a lot of guessing.

The employee is on alert because of the boss' unclear communication. The employee also interprets this as the boss not liking them, which plants a seed of a threat in their mind. The employee feels this threat as a potential loss of their job, reputation, career, or financial security.

The boss picks up this dysregulation in the employee and takes it as a personal threat to their authority. Maybe they feel fear, loss of reputation, or lack of subordination, and respond by trying to be more controlling. They may create more unpredictability.

In the meantime, the employee becomes more dysregulated, fears communicating with the boss, and their coworkers pick up on the dysregulation. The work environment becomes dysregulated as the stress spreads contagiously through lack of communication, trust, and honesty. The employees feel a cloud of unsafety, and they become more and more dysregulated as they do not know if their jobs are at risk. This cloud of uncertainty creates a disconnect in the environment and the employees come to work feeling unwelcome and uncertain every day.

Other Scenarios

Yesterday I read an article that was written by a mother of a teenage boy. She said that her son slammed the door in anger, causing the mirror to fall of the wall and shatter. Her initial reaction was anger. She was furious, and her first thought was to go and yell at her son for what he had done and the damage he had created. She decided to go outside and cool off first.

When she was outside, she could hear her son crying from the open bathroom window. The sound of his sobs shifted something inside of her. She no longer perceived her son's action as a threat, but for what it was: pain. Something had hurt him and he reacted in the stress response. Because of this, she was able to calmly address him with love and not escalate the situation. She felt compassion instead of fear, which is the key antidote to the stress response.

Fear is contagious, but so is empathy. Fear and panic evolved as a survival mechanism in our brains to keep us safe. But instead of letting them be in charge, we can now understand the purpose they serve and respond with compassion.

Reflection:

Describe a scenario where a dysregulated person's stress response became contagious.

_____

_____

_____

_____

_____

7
THE EFFECTS OF CONSTANT DYSREGULATION

If you work or live in a high stress environment, stress can put you at risk for communication problems and burnout. In this chapter, we are going to talk about some of the short-term and long-term effects of being frequently dysregulated.

The Short-Term Effects of Dysregulation

Being dysregulated or in a constant state of alarm triggers the release of the stress hormones adrenaline and cortisol. The purpose of this flood of hormones is to give you the energy and power you may need to fight off a predator or quickly run away.

Because of this, your heart rate increases, your blood pressure elevates, and your breathing may become quickened or shallow. You may feel shaky or sweaty. You may find it difficult to concentrate and experience short-term memory problems.

Due to the difficulties in concentrating, you may make errors in your work or in your judgment, or you may find yourself being short tempered with everyone you interact with. Remember, when you are dysregulated, you do not have full access to your cortex. Mistakes are made and miscommunication occurs.

This constant state of dysregulation and agitation could make it difficult to fall asleep because you may feel too hyped up on the constant flow of stress hormones running through your bloodstream. This can start a roller coaster ride of the insomnia/sleep deprivation cycle, which just leads to more sleep deprivation and more dysregulation.

Your appetite may increase or decrease dramatically. Some people may skip meals, while others may try to sooth themselves with food, specifically junk foods that are high in sugar or fat. This can lead to weight changes, which over time can cause other health issues.

As you remain in a constant state of unmanaged stress or dysregulation, you may notice yourself becoming more reactive to minor, perceived threats. This shorter temper is hypervigilance. This is the body's way of always being prepared to fight or run. You will be on the lookout for more threats in your day to day life, and your threshold for normal stress will become lower and lower.

This daily stress has now turned into chronic dysregulation. Your personal and professional relationships may suffer as you lash out at those closest to you, which creates even more tension and communication problems. These are the beginning stages of burnout.

Constant dysregulation can cause:

- Burnout
- Compassion Fatigue
- Acne
- Chronic Pain
- Frequent illness/immune problems
- Decreased Energy
- Insomnia
- Appetite and digestive issues
- Relationship & communication problems
- Inflammation
- Weight gain

Long-term Health Effects of Dysregulation

When the stress remains chronic and unmanaged for long periods of time, the body's inflammatory response will be triggered by the constant flood of stress hormones flowing through your body. Over the years, chronic stress can be linked to heart attacks, stroke, diabetes, cancer, a weakened immune function, mental health issues, and a general lack of energy.

Constant dysregulation can make you vulnerable to all the negative health outcomes that we discussed surrounding the ACE study and the long-term impact of childhood trauma. They may or may not be as severe as if they happened in childhood while the brain was developing, but the brain can create new neural pathways when exposed to constant stress hyper vigilance for long periods of time.

Does this mean I have to quit my job?

No. If everyone who worked in a high stress position quit because of chronic stress, we would have no teachers, doctors, nurses, or first responders. In the next part of this book, we are going to talk about some ways to counteract this chronic stress. I believe that the best ways to counteract the negative effects of chronic stress and dysregulation are to:

1. Understand how the survival brain works, what your stress response and triggers are, and understand the stress response and triggers of others.

2. Understanding arguments, tantrums, and miscommunication as a stress response rather than taking it as a personal attack.

3. Self-regulate so that you can bring the calm, regulated energy to whatever situation you find yourself in.

Now that we have discussed what it means to be dysregulated and how it happens, we are going to talk about regulation.

8
REGULATION

In the previous chapters, we learned about the brain, how the stress response works, and the effects of stress and dysregulation. Now that you have that foundation, this chapter is going to teach you how to self-regulate, how to help a dysregulated person become regulated, and how to create a regulated, calm environment.

How to Self-Regulate

This section may be the most important in this entire book. The reason is this: ***Regulated people can set the tone for those around them, like a thermostat.*** This is especially true for people in positions of authority such as corporate leaders, school administrators, teachers, doctors, nurses, and parents. Leaders set the tone. If a leader is dysregulated, chaos ensues. If a leader is regulated, rational discourse and problem solving is possible.

If you are dysregulated, you will feel many of the negative physical and emotional effects that we discussed in Chapter 4 and it will be harder to communicate with others, especially if they are also dysregulated or become dysregulated by catching your stress. This is true for all interactions. However, if you understand how to regulate yourself, there is a strong likelihood that you will lower your own overall stress levels and their negative effects. You may find more peace, joy and calm within yourself, and you will have better access to your cortex, the thinking part of your brain. This will benefit all the people you interact with, especially if you are a leader. You will be better equipped to serve others and help them stay regulated in stressful situations.

How to notice your dysregulation patterns- the first step to self-regulation

1. Understand the brain/body connection. When your "survival brain" kicks in, your "thinking brain" may not be accessible.
2. Start noticing the signs of becoming dysregulated. Becoming dysregulated looks and feels different for all of us. Below, I have listed some common signs of dysregulation. There may be others that are not included in the list.

Common Signs That a Person is Dysregulated

- Losing temper
- Becoming argumentative or defensive
- Becoming violent
- Swearing
- Leaving the situation abruptly or running away
- Increased heart rate or blood pressure
- Feeling flushed
- Feeling sweaty
- Feeling the need to tap or create rhythm
- Losing concentration or the ability to think clearly
- Feeling the need to withdraw or escape
- Feeling like you are going to cry
- Change in voice tone, speed, or volume
- Feeling the need to pace or move around

- Feeling the need to overeat, drink, smoke, or medicate
- Completely shutting down
- Feeling nervous or anxious
- The need to hide or escape to fantasy world in book, tv or video games

After noticing your own personal signs that you may be becoming dysregulated, would you say they align more with FIGHT, FLIGHT, or FREEZE?

3. Identify your triggers

Now that you have become aware of the signs of dysregulation in your body, try to notice when these signs occur for you. These may be considered your "triggers" and can be different for everyone. Some common triggers include:

- Being criticized or judged
- Being in an unfamiliar situation
- Meeting a new person
- Not getting enough sleep
- Reacting to someone else who is agitated or dysregulated
- Feeling pressured by oneself or by others
- Being questioned on one's professionalism, authority, knowledge, ability, or expertise.

Keep in mind, triggers vary from person to person and we all have different levels of sensitivity to stress, partly due to our own developmental backgrounds, trauma history, and personal resilience factors. This greatly impacts what our survival brain associates with a threat.

Reflection:

What are your stress response triggers?

_____

_____

_____

_____

_____

Why do you think these triggers make you feel threatened?

_____

_____

_____

_____

Now that you understand the survival brain, your own signs of dysregulation, and some of your general triggers, we can talk about how to keep yourself regulated and self-regulate when you recognize the early stages of dysregulation.

How to Self-Regulate:

1. Add Rhythm

Remember when we talked about how the brainstem develops in utero? While the brainstem is developing, there is the constant rhythm of the mother's heartbeat. The brainstem associates this rhythm with safety, as a developing baby is in a completely safe environment where all it's needs are being met. Rhythm keeps us regulated. This is the reason rocking, patting, and singing soothe distressed babies.

Here are some ways you can add rhythm to your life. Add more as you think of them:

- Walking or pacing
- Rocking chairs or swings
- Driving
- Music
- Singing
- Bouncing or dribbling a ball
- Knitting, drawing, coloring, painting

If you feel yourself starting to get dysregulated, try to add some rhythm.

2. Make sure your survival needs are being fully met.

- Are you getting enough sleep and rest?
- Are you eating regularly?
- Are you drinking enough water?
- Do you have strong connections with supportive people who listen to you?

In our sleep-deprived world, it may seem difficult to get enough rest all the time. Being aware that sleep deprivation puts you into a state of dysregulation can help you to be mindful to get enough sleep so that you don't start off the day dysregulated.

3. Movement & Breaks

Movement is another vital key to staying regulated. The brain needs sufficient movement and does not like to concentrate for long periods of time on the same thing. Breaks are essential. Studies have shown that the quality of a person's work decreases the longer they are sitting or working on a concentrated task. The longer you go without a break or without some movement, the more likely you are to become dysregulated. If working for long periods without a break is common for you, you may be dysregulated and not even realize it. Working too long without a break can be a trigger for dysregulation. This is one reason kids have recess; it is essential for learning and concentration.

Reflection:

What are some ways you can add movement to your day?

_____

_____

_____

_____

_____

4. Add Predictability as much as possible.

Routines & Procedures

As we have learned, the survival brain filters anything that is unfamiliar as unsafe. For this reason, we may feel nervous when we are faced with uncertainty in all areas of life. If your work or areas of your life involve a lot of unpredictability or uncertainty, it can help to create some anchoring routines or some form of predictability throughout your day.

If certain parts of your day feel chaotic, it's possible that a procedure could help. When I was a teacher, it helped the students and myself to have procedures for every part of the day. This always helped all of us know exactly what we needed to do and took the uncertainty out of parts of the day that could get chaotic. We had a procedure for check-in, a procedure for how to have a group discussion, a procedure for turning in assignments. The procedures helped the students feel safe because they always knew what was expected of them. Think about flying on an airplane. There is a procedure for checking luggage, boarding the plane, finding your seat, etc. When you fly, you always know the procedures for each step of the trip. Procedures take the guesswork out of how you show up and give some sense of predictability.

Reflection:

What are some ways you can add predictability or routine to your personal or professional life?

_____
_____
_____
_____
_____

What are some ways you can create procedures or predictability in the most unpredictable parts of your day or life?

_____
_____
_____
_____
_____

5. Connection

Relationships are the #1 key to staying regulated. The most resilient people have the most connective, caring relationships. I would say that connective, caring relationships are the key to everything in life. If you have regulated, caring people surrounding you, they can listen to you when you start to feel dysregulated.

I also think that connection with your SELF is vital to staying regulated. Self-connection helps you become more self-aware, which will naturally help you stay self-regulated. Being connected to your intuition, inner wisdom, higher power, or God, is also a very helpful component to staying regulated. Some ways to connect with this spiritual element include journaling, meditating, prayer, and being in nature.

Walk and talks are some of the best ways to stay regulated because they combine walking (movement and rhythm) with talking and listening (connection). Add walk and talks to your routine, and you will also add predictability.

6. Fun & Meaning

When your day feels fun, meaningful, and rewarding, you will feel more regulated. I think that connection plus fun is rewarding, so it is intrinsically motivating. When seriousness or heaviness takes over, it's harder to stay regulated. Lighten up the mood with fun on a regular basis and it will be easier to stay regulated.

Recap on How to Stay Regulated:

1. Add Rhythm

2. Make sure your survival needs are met

3. Add movement and breaks

4. Add predictability

5. Add connections

6. Add fun and meaning

How To Get Regulated When You Become Dysregulated

1. Recognize that your survival brain has been activated. Do NOT try to "think" your way out of it. PAUSE, and take some deep breaths. Recognize that your survival brain has picked up on something and is trying to keep you safe. It might be possible to identify what triggered you, but this is less important than recognizing that you are getting dysregulated.

2. If possible, excuse yourself from the situation. Take a break or take a walk.

This will remove you from the trigger, which will remove the threat. If this is not possible and you must stay, try to take deep, focused breaths until you feel yourself becoming calm.

Remember, your body will feel the stress of the trigger and you do not have full access to your cortex at this time. Try to regulate your body before making any decisions or saying anything you may regret. Focus on regulating your body.

When you are dysregulated, try to add movement, rhythm and connection with a regulated person to your situation.

Take a walk, take some focused breaths, and call a friend.

When your body feels calmer you will be better able to think clearly. Then you may want to ask yourself:

- What triggered you? Can you identify it? Why does this feel like a threat to you?
- How can you prevent this type of stress response in the future?

Depending on how self-aware you want to become, identifying your triggers could be useful to staying more self-regulated and happier overall. I recommend using the above questions as journal prompts to help yourself understand and get more connected with your intuition.

Sometimes, people try and regulate in ways that tend to be harmful to themselves and others. Some common and potentially harmful ways that people self-regulate include:

- Drugs
- Alcohol
- Smoking

- Overeating
- Driving too fast
- Reckless or high-risk behavior

Oftentimes when people engage with harmful self-regulating tactics, it is because they are in the stress response without realizing it.

Hopefully you understand more about how to regulate yourself and minimize incidences of becoming dysregulated. This knowledge can improve your life in all areas and the more you *practice* self-regulation the more self-aware you will become. Remember, this is about the process, not perfection. Little by little, day by day, your self-awareness will expand as you put this information and learning to use in the situations that will eventually crop up in your life. It can be life changing.

Don't worry if you still get dysregulated. It happens to us all. Each time it happens, you can learn more about yourself by asking:

1. Why did this happen?

2. What do I need to understand to prevent this from happening in the future?

Each time you ask these questions, you will learn more about yourself and become better able to communicate with others.

How to Help Regulate a Dysregulated Person

Now that you have read about how to stay regulated and to regulate yourself when you get dysregulated, we are going to talk about ways you can help regulate another dysregulated person. It's important to understand how to keep yourself regulated before trying to regulate a dysregulated person because the best way to regulate a dysregulated person is be regulated yourself as you interact with them.

This is especially true when you are a leader or in a position of authority. Remember, the leader controls the "thermostat."

It is also true that if you are dysregulated you can cause someone else to become dysregulated and fearful. This means the primary goal is to BE self-regulated. Bring the calm. Once you are regulated, do the following steps.

1. Physical Regulation:

Try to give this person something that can provide **physical** regulation. This could be something that provides rhythm or movement, or it could be a cold drink of water, a snack, or piece of candy. You could even try humming, singing, or swaying near the person. If it is a child, offer something to draw or color or something to touch like a stuffed animal or a piece of clay. If you know the person, ask if they want to take a walk with you. The key here is to offer them something that will physically regulate them.

Remember, the person does not have access to their cortex when they are dysregulated. They will not be able to have a rational conversation with you at this time about anything.

DO NOT try to ask them questions in any way, especially about why they are dysregulated.

DO NOT try to touch them or they may react violently.

Just stay quiet and present, without getting too close into their space.

Try This:	Avoid:
• Music or Rhythm • Swaying, tapping, humming • Offering a snack or drink • Deep breathing exercises together • Offer to take them for a walk if possible	• Asking Questions • Talking • Criticizing • Direct eye contact • Getting too close in a threatening way • Especially avoid physical contact if you do not know the person well • NEVER say "Calm Down"

The mistake many of us make is we try to engage the dysregulated person in conversation. We start to try to talk to them or ask questions about what's wrong. Worse yet, we start giving orders, suggestions, or recommendations and say things like, "calm down," or "why are you acting like this?"

Trying to control the situation also makes it more likely that you will "catch" their stress.

Sometimes, if possible, it is best to give the dysregulated person some space. If they are open to anything physically regulating, give it to them. If you are close to them, try to get beside them rather than across from them, which can be perceived as threatening. Stay silent. Let them be the one to talk if they decide. The most important thing you can do here is stay calm and regulated.

The best thing that I ever did with dysregulated students who were in the fight or flight mode was to simply say, "Do you want to walk with me?" They usually wanted to go. I would take them for a walk in the hallway, side by side. We would walk laps and I remained SILENT, even if they started talking, which usually happened. Many of the students had just been on the verge of a fight or meltdown or had run out of their classroom. I did not try to talk to them. I just calmly offered the space for a walk and walked beside them silently.

My silence gave them a sense of safety, and the rhythm and movement of the walking started to regulate their body and brain. They almost always started talking, sometimes fearfully and fast, about whatever had happened. Often it didn't make sense, as they weren't able to think clearly yet. As we walked and walked, they got calmer and calmer, and were able to think more clearly. As they calmed down, access to their cortex was restored and they were able to process what had happened and what had triggered their stress response.

2. Connect:

Once the person is calm and regulated, the next step is to establish some sort of connection. I think that walk and talks are so magical because they provide the movement, rhythm and connection all in one. The connection should provide the person with a sense of safety, as if you are there by their side. This works best if you can actually be there next to them, avoiding intense eye contact. Remember, they still may not have full access to their cortex (thinking, rational, decision-making brain), so try to keep any conversation on something light, and not related to their stressor unless they want to talk about it.

Recap of Key Points

- Go side by side/next to the person
- If you speak, make sure your voice is calm and only speak in response to them

The dysregulated person will only feel safe if they think you care about them. If they perceive you as a threat in any way, they may stay dysregulated. The way that I showed my caring with dysregulated students was to simply be there for them, understanding they were in crisis.

Ideas to connect with a dysregulated person and help them feel safe:

- Get side by side, which is empowering vs. face to face, which can feel threatening or controlling
- Listen with understanding
- Listen more than speaking
- Offer reassurance that you will do your best to help them

3. Talk about it

Once the person is calm and regulated and has regained access to their cortex, you can probably have a discussion with them.

With students, this was key because the point of my job was to teach them self-regulation skills so they could learn ways to manage their stress response and stay in school, avoiding suspension. But for me, my job had a deeper meaning. I wanted to make sure they knew and understood that they weren't "bad kids" as they were so often labeled. So, after they were physically regulated and we had connected and developed trust, we were able to talk about it.

Now that they had regained full access to their cortex, we could talk about what happened and why they felt threatened. But more importantly, we were able to talk about the stress response and how it was their survival brain's way of keeping them safe. I felt this was important so that the trauma didn't get turned into shame. I didn't want them to feel like something was wrong with them; I wanted them to understand that their brain was trying to protect them. From that understanding, we could talk about things they could do in the future to self-regulate.

4. Practice

The fourth step is practice. I would be at school to remind students of their new skills and be there to support them as they practiced self-regulating. It takes practice to learn how to stop reacting in a stress response and take care of one's self.

A Recap of the Steps to Helping A Dysregulated Person Regulate (De-escalation)

1. Physical Regulation

2. Connect/Establish trust

3. After the person is regulated, then you can talk about it

4. Practice skills

9
HOW TO CREATE A REGULATED ENVIRONMENT FOR LEADERS

Now that you know how to keep yourself regulated and help calm a dysregulated person, let's talk about creating a regulated environment. As we discussed before, our mirror neurons can pick up the energy or mood of our environment, and the more calm, regulated people there are in the environment, the more the calm energy will be contagious.

Energy snowballs in either direction:

>Dysregulated energy multiplies into CHAOS.

>Regulated energy multiplies into CALM.

There are ways that we can help to create a calmer, more regulated environment. Obviously, we cannot control all the factors, especially in higher stress environments such as emergency rooms. However, there are many factors that we can control, which can help bring calm to these high stress environments. These factors will bring an overall "regulated" energy to the environment. Many of them are the same factors that we use to keep ourselves self-regulated.

1. Predictability

As we know, the brain is always on the lookout for familiar (safe) or unfamiliar (unsafe). The more predictability you can bring into the environment, the safer everyone will feel. Below are some examples.

- Giving clear expectations and rules of the environment
- Having simple, clear procedures and routines
- Giving notice of anything out of the ordinary that will be happening
- Clear boundaries and agreements with all members involved in the environment

This will obviously vary from situation to situation, but the point is, people get dysregulated when they are caught off guard or don't know what is expected of them. Eliminating surprises will increase the sense of safety.

Reflection:

1. How can you create predictability in your environment?

_____

_____

_____

_____

_____

2. Where in your environment do you feel unpredictability?

_____

_____

_____

_____

_____

3. Where do you experience unpredictability in your interactions/communications?

_____
_____
_____
_____
_____

4. Where could you add some routines or procedures to increase safety?

_____
_____
_____
_____
_____

5. Where could you create boundaries and agreements with people in your environment to create predictability about expectations?

_____
_____
_____
_____
_____

2. Rhythm, Movement and Breaks

Adding music, rhythm, movement and breaks is essential to keeping everyone in the space regulated. Many work environments discourage employees from taking frequent breaks, but taking breaks actually increases productivity.

What are some ways you can incorporate rhythm, breaks or music into your workday?

_____

_____

_____

_____

3. Respectful Connections: Culture of Respect

Relationship safety is the number one factor in keeping people regulated. Respect is also contagious. When people feel safe and respected, there is a sense of connection in the environment. When people feel disrespected, there is a sense of danger and disconnection in the environment.

When leaders are respectful and communicate honestly, the environment will feel connected and positive. There will be more connective, respectful, working relationships, and this energy will be felt by everyone in the environment.

However, if there is some disrespect or disconnect with the environment or among leadership, this will be felt by everyone in the system or environment. These types of things trickle down and poison the system, no matter how well hidden the leaders at the top believe them to be. This type of stress contagion will be felt everywhere in the environment and there will be a higher likelihood of dysregulation among those involved.

A respectful, regulated environment is one in which:

- Everyone feels seen and heard
- Everyone feels treated like a valuable human being, rather than a number or obligation

- Everyone feels they have choices and are free to make decisions for themselves without fear of punishment or loss of security
- Everyone feels safe to voice their concerns without punishment or loss of safety

The systems-wide approach is the best way to create a regulated environment and would be the optimal way to make sure there is a sense of honest, open, respectful connection and communication. In this approach, everyone understands how to self-regulate and understands the way our stress response works so they don't take dysregulation personally. This could transform your environment.

The person in charge sets the tone. Are you setting a tone of safety and respect? Or a tone of fear?

Remember that actions always speak louder than words. Our brains pick up on the energy behind your words, rather than the words themselves, especially when we are used to being on alert for danger.

Actions that set the tone for respect and connection:

- Acknowledge everyone involved; respectfully greet them by name. People want to know that you see them.
- Remove all feelings of hierarchy and the need to control members of your environment.
- Ask people their opinions and what they think on a regular basis. Show them that their ideas and opinions matter.
- Look for opportunities to connect and have human-to-human interactions rather than only focusing on getting the job done.

For any person working in a high stress situation, it is key to remember WHY you are doing this work. Connect with yourself and remember your purpose for doing the work you do.

Reflection:

1. How can you show the people in your environment that they are seen and heard and that you care about them?

_____

_____

_____

_____

2. How can you let the people you work with know that you respect and value them rather than seeing them as a number or obligation?

_____

_____

_____

_____

3. Where do you feel you have choices in your environment? Where do you feel you have no choices?

_____

_____

_____

_____

4. How can you give those you lead choices and the freedom to make decisions for themselves?

_____

_____

_____

_____

_____

5. How can you show those you lead that they are safe to voice their concerns?

_____

_____

_____

_____

_____

6. Why is your work (as a leader) meaningful to you?

_____

_____

_____

_____

_____

10

EMPATHY IS THE ANTIDOTE TO THE STRESS RESPONSE

In this chapter, I would like to focus on empathy.

Empathy is simply the ability to understand and share the feelings of another person.

Empathy is the antidote to the stress response. Dysregulation can spread, but so can calm. I wanted to write this book to provide some understanding on what happens in the brain and body when a person shows signs of dysregulation, which is the body's natural stress response. I believe that with this perspective and understanding, you can have more empathy for everyone in your life, including yourself. You can now take stress response & dysregulation less personally, and be able to:

- Self-regulate

- Have more self-awareness

- Develop your intuition

- Understand others when they are in the vulnerable state of survival mode

I believe relationships are the most important part of life, professionally and personally. When you understand the brain and stress response, it opens an entirely enlightened perspective, rather than the old worn out stories we tell ourselves when we take people's anger, frustration, or fear personally. It offers a different perspective.

This knowledge can empower us. Now, instead of taking the fear reactions personally, we can stay calm and choose to stay regulated, rather than reacting with our own fear response. Instead of reacting with fear, we have awareness that allows us the choice of deciding how to respond. This knowledge and understanding empowers us to rise above our basic survival mode and elevates us to a position of powerful choice – the choice to see our purpose and deeper meaning in the connections with those we are interacting with.

I believe we came here to connect, relate and serve others, not just survive, react, and be stuck in fear. With this knowledge, we no longer have to take another person's reactions personally, and this can transform every part of our lives. Our personal and professional relationships will improve.

Now, instead of just surviving, we can thrive in ways that make us uniquely human. We have the ability to love, empathize, and create all types of meaningful relationships. I also believe that this understanding will bring us closer to being able to listen to our own intuition, which has possibly been "cluttered up" and clouded by misunderstandings.

Reflection:

How can understanding the brain and stress response help you to understand your emotions and reactions?

_____

_____

_____

_____

_____

How can understanding the brain and stress response help you to understand other people's emotional reactions?

_____

_____

_____

_____

How can understanding the brain and stress response change the way you interact with people?

_____

_____

_____

_____

How can understanding the brain and stress response help you create a safer, more respectful environment?

_____

_____

_____

_____

In what ways do you think understanding the stress response can help you reduce your own stress?

_____

_____

_____

_____

In what ways do you think understanding the stress response will increase your capacity for empathy?

_____

_____

_____

_____

11
PUNISHING STUDENTS FOR TRAUMA RESPONSES CREATES MORE STRESS AND TRAUMA

Punishing students for their stress response creates more trauma and stress, while teaching students about their brains and the skills to self-regulate creates calm, safe, respectful learning environments.

I worked with a teacher who told me a story that illustrates how simply teaching a student how to self-regulate can build a relationship with the student, teach the student valuable self-regulation skills that will serve them in every area of their life, and show them that you believe they are a valuable human being who deserves to be respected and understood.

Frank's story

Frank is a middle school teacher who worked with me as a coachee. The focus of our coaching work together included developing stronger relationships with students and teaching his students self-regulation skills to improve classroom behavior. We began working together because Frank had become so overwhelmed with "discipline" issues he didn't know if he could continue being a teacher.

After learning about the stress response and dysregulation, Frank started to see that the root most of the "behavior problems" in his school were because teachers didn't understand the brain and stress response and students were completely unaware of the way their brains and stress response worked.

Frank developed a rapport with a student who appeared to be dysregulated during a large school assembly in the gym during the first two weeks of the school year. He noticed that she was wiggling around, talking loudly, and about to become disruptive. Frank had been working hard to learn all about the brain, trauma, the stress response, and ways he could serve his students better, so when he noticed that the student appeared to be getting dysregulated, he said, "Come on, let's go for a walk." He took the student and her friend out into the hallway to walk back and forth through the empty halls. He didn't really talk to them at all, just gave them a chance to regulate, as he knew that large assemblies and crowded gatherings could be stress triggers for some students.

Frank had been working with me long enough to know that when a student starts to get dysregulated, it usually shows up as misbehavior or acting out.

The most important thing the teacher or adult can do in this situation is to listen and truly hear the student by being present. This is not the time for lectures, criticizing, or judgment. After this deep listening occurs, the teacher or adult can start asking questions to get to the root of what happened. Then, the adult must help the student learn what to do the next time a situation like that occurs. The teacher needs to coach the student on how to respond to stress and to self-regulate, rather than just react to the stress response. Ideally, the teacher would also give the student a chance to practice the new skill with some repetition.)

Frank took the students into the hall, walked with them, and taught them about the brain and being dysregulated. He told them that walking and taking a quick break were ways to self-regulate. This positive interaction created a great rapport, as the students felt heard, seen, and understood. Also, the students felt like they could understand themselves better.

Three weeks later during middle school recess where students get to sit on the bleachers or play games in the gym after lunch, Frank noticed the student from the assembly and described her as looking like she was "about to blow a gasket." Just as he was about to approach her to see if she would like to take a "regulation break," his colleague confronted the student and told her to sit still, not to talk, and to serve her detention." This caused the student to become more dysregulated, as she visibly became angrier.

Frank approached his colleague, Ms. DiMarco, who had "recess duty" and asked, "Can I take her for a walk?" She replied, "No, she cannot walk. She has to serve her detention for Mr. Smith. She disrespected him and now must serve detention."

The student was about to lose it, and Frank decided he might have to override Ms. DiMarco and just take the student for a walk before she had a complete meltdown. He asked once more time and his colleague finally agreed. She said, "just one lap."

Frank took the student and walked in silence. She was very angry, and at first talked about how she was mad at Mr. Smith and Ms. DiMarco, but eventually calmed down. Frank was able to reason with the student, and she decided that she wanted to remedy the situation with Mr. Smith by having a discussion with him. She wanted to apologize to him for appearing disrespectful, and eventually explained that she had had a very bad morning at home before school and her mood had made her a bit short tempered. This simple, understanding interaction created a better rapport with the student, Frank, and Mr. Smith, who now understood the student better. It taught the student self-regulation skills, communication skills, and ways to ask for help the next time she feels herself getting dysregulated.

Frank's question for me was this: Why was Ms. DiMarco so rigid with her need to stick with the punishment? He said, "She was being so tough about it, even though the student was obviously distressed."

My answer to Frank came out looking like this:

Traditional or "Institutional" Schooling:	Trauma-Sensitive Schooling:
• "Tough Love" (teacher and staff think they need to be "tough" with students to "keep control."	• Love, empathy and understanding
• Harsh rules and discipline	• Clear expectations and agreements
• Punish students for natural stress response reactions	• Understand the stress response and teach students self-regulation skills.
• Creates a separation and power differential between teachers and students.	• Equity and Respect
• Need to have control and power over the students	• Teacher empowers students by teaching self-regulation and self-control.
• Assumes students aren't trustworthy and/or are "bad"	• Trusts students and believes they are all inherently "good."
• "Bad" students act out because they are "disrespectful" and have malicious intent.	• Knows that all people can get dysregulated, and people who have experienced high levels of trauma can have a more highly sensitized stress response.
• Assume students have self-regulation skills but choose not to use them.	• Understands that all students need to be taught self-regulation skills. Teaches skills and helps students practice new skills in stressful situations.

• Creates separation between students and teachers	• Cultivates respectful relationships between students and teachers, and other students
• Does not examine implicit or subconscious biases	• Examines subconscious and implicit biases and practices continuous awareness of how they can show up in support of students.
• Believes schools primarily exist to teach subject matter. Overly concerned with academics or performance.	• Believes schools should teach humans first, then subject matter. Primarily concerned with the overall wellbeing of students and teachers.

There is a printable version of this on my website at https://christinarenzelli.com/creatingcalm.

Most people want to "do good." Often, the harmful, systemic beliefs and practices of a "traditional" schooling environment can infect the mind of the most optimistic, kind-hearted of teachers. This happens especially when teachers are brand new and starving for mentors or someone who will help them to survive their first difficult years. It's almost like they just adapt to the attitudes and beliefs of the poisonous thoughts around them for survival.

"Most of us want to do good, but sometimes we don't know how."

This was my response to Layla, a teacher I had been coaching when she told me a story of how she accidentally overheard a school administrator lecturing a parent on the topic of "respect". Layla said the principal basically tore into the parent, criticizing and judging her parenting skills and her child. Ironically, as he lectured about the "importance of teaching respect," he did exactly the opposite in modeling true respect. Layla said she just didn't understand why the administrator was "laying into" the parent in such a "disrespectful" way. "Couldn't he see that he was not being respectful to the parent?" It was obvious to Layla that this was a condescending and degrading lecture, not a respectful, useful, empowering conversation. "And he (the administrator) is really a good guy. Why did he do all that?"

My response was, "People want to do good, but sometimes they don't know how."

Layla laughed and said, "THAT quote is going to be the first slide of my presentation." She was doing a presentation on behavior management for the discipline committee and her number one obstacle was to convince the teachers that students want to do well; we just have to teach them the skills to do so. Layla had been working with me for over a year and was starting to notice how her peers were adopting the negative biases against the students that seemed to be the norm in the school building.

The administrator was demonstrating the same situation as students who don't know how to self-regulate or handle a situation. He wasn't exactly sure how to self-regulate, given the stressed tone of his lecture, and he didn't know how to connect with the parent in order to actually communicate in a productive way. I've seen it over and over in schools – the lecturing, condescending way that some administrators speak to the students. They are not trying to be condescending or ineffective, it is just the way they were probably parented or schooled, but it is also the way that traditional schools relate to students. It is the "power over" model that creates more disconnection.

If we don't examine our belief system, we will parent the way we were parented, and we will teach the way we were taught. And when it comes to classroom management, we will use the same technique our parents or teachers used with us. This can be a problem.

My theory is that most school or classroom behavior issues can be traced back to the stress response and lack of self-regulation skills as well as the lack of a trusting connection with the leader or teacher. Classroom management is rarely taught in college education classes even though it is the foundation to creating an optimal learning environment.

Children don't usually know how to self-regulate. They must be taught self-regulation skills. The problem is many adults do not know how to self-regulate either and therefore are not equipped to teach their students self-regulation skills. If adults don't know to self-regulate, how can we fully teach our kids?

We expect them to "just know," just as we are expected to "just know." It doesn't always work this way and the results can be disastrous.

Reflection

Look at the chart provided on Traditional versus Trauma-Sensitive Schools. Would you say your school falls into the "Traditional" side of the chart, or the "Trauma-Sensitive" side of the chart?

_____

_____

_____

_____

_____

How do you think you will shift your thinking after reading the story or chart in this chapter? What impact has this chapter had on your perspective?

_____

_____

_____

_____

_____

What are some ideas you have about this knowledge that can help you in your journey as an educator?

_____

_____

_____

_____

_____

12

SCHOOLS CAN TRANSFORM LIVES OR CRUSH SOULS

> "Let your face speak what's in your heart. When they walk in the room my face says I'm glad to see them. It's just as small as that, you see?" -Toni Morrison

I've been to a lot of schools in my lifetime as a teacher and coach, and they all have their own unique energy about them. The same is true for every office or workplace I've ever been in. The reason for this is: ***energy is contagious***.

Anyone that's ever had to be in charge of a classroom or group of people knows that the snowball effect is real. There is a certain mood to the cycles of the days, weeks, and months of the school year. A Monday morning feels much different than a chaotic Friday afternoon. Part of it is mood and excitement, but a lot of it is mirror neurons.

Most of us know what it feels like to be around someone who may not like us. It doesn't feel great, and if you've ever experienced it, you know that you start to mirror back feelings of dislike for that person, no matter how enlightened of a person you may be. Think back to a time in your life where you encountered someone who you felt did not like you, or at least had some negativity towards you. How did you feel? How did you react?

Now hopefully you have also experienced a person who adored you. I hope that every person gets to experience the feeling, at least once in their life, of making someone's "eyes light up" when you enter the room.

This is the feeling that I had with my grandmother. Her name was Pearl and she adored me and my sisters. She was also a school cook and custodian, known as "Miss Pearl" to the students. She adored the children at school, and all of them knew that she cared about them. She had a massive collection of school pictures from students over the years. They all had notes of love and appreciation written on the backs of the photos. There is nothing quite as good as the feeling of making someone's eyes light up just by your presence. My Grandma Pearl was one of the most influential and important people in my life. She shaped my entire teaching career. I decided that I wanted my students to feel the way I felt when I was with my grandma, even if it was on more of a professional, teacher/student level. This can transform a classroom and a school. This tells students that they are lovable and they matter and we see them. It shows them that they are valued. They feel it in their hearts when their teachers' eyes light up.

Now, let's be honest, many schools are not like this and there are plenty of reasons for that. Toxic stress, trauma, exhaustion, boredom, and chaos are just some of the reasons that teachers, principals, and school staff's eyes do not light up when they are in the presence of their students. But this is a vicious cycle that I believe can be solved by deciding to change or shift your perspective. When schools are too tired, overwhelmed, or exhausted to bring this spark of love to the atmosphere, kids feel it. And when kids feel it, they mirror it. Kids will reflect the mindset of their leader.

Take a look at your students and decide that your eyes are going to light up when you see them. When a child feels like an adult adores them, sees them for being a lovable, imperfectly perfect human, their eyes will light up, reflecting the same love, and then these mirror neurons will snowball in the loving, positive direction. This can transform a school. It can transform a life and can transform many lives. This is what transforms the world. My Grandma Pearl's simple, honest love and adoration can transform the world.

IT ALL STARTS WITH BELIEFS

"My teacher thought I was smarter than I was, so I was." -Anonymous

Teachers are authority figures. No matter the student's situation, they regard teachers as knowing everything, or almost everything. If a student thinks that you, the teacher, believe that they are "bad," or "good" they are going to believe you, regardless of the truth in that belief. Teachers have such power to mold minds that we need to be mindful of our own beliefs, opinions, and stereotypes, ESPECIALLY when students are showing behaviors that are not ideal, and especially when students become dysregulated.

When teachers and school staff believe negative thoughts about their students and then talk or even think about how bad, rotten, and terminally hopeless their students are, kids feel it. And then their actions reflect these feelings and beliefs. Your eyes may be the only adult eyes they see all day. Isn't it worth it to light them up for that child, no matter how distasteful you may think they are or how much stress they may have put you through? I promise, it is worth it. Don't take their behavior personally.

We have a choice. You get to decide. Are your students good, or are they bad?

Schools that have a more negative energy or tone can be especially poisonous to fresh new teachers who are coming in to "save the world." I'm telling you this so you can set yourself up with some immunity, before you become unsuspectingly poisoned.

Start keeping your eyes and ears open for negative comments or actions that reflect negative beliefs about students, because these beliefs can be contagious and damaging. This is especially important in schools with higher trauma. Kids who have experienced trauma and toxic stress are going to come in with a higher sensitivity to potential threats. If they see fear in you, they are going to feel fear in themselves, and this is the opposite of positive. This will trigger the response of fight, flight, or freeze.

Contagious negative beliefs about students will create an unsafe, toxic environment. This can make it difficult to maintain positive, loving beliefs when a teacher is new, with nothing to compare it to.

"Badness" is a mind virus around schools, especially schools that are higher poverty and higher stress. The "bad" kids quickly get labelled, and then often times live up to their labels. These are our most vulnerable children, and usually have experienced nightmarish situations that teachers may or may not be fully aware of, which is causing them to "act out" by fighting, fleeing or shutting down. When the school, teachers or administrators label them as "bad," (or even hold this belief), students take this on as part of their identity and oftentimes wear it all through life, even onto prison. This toxic shame, this belief of "I am bad" can often create a self-fulfilling prophecy.

This, I believe is the true school to prison pipeline. In reality, the children that get in trouble or who are labeled as bad, need our help the most. They need our full, listening attention. They need us to hear and understand what is causing them to get "dysregulated," and then to "get in trouble" so we can teach them self-regulation skills. This is why suspension is the WORST thing we can do.

What you believe sets the foundation for everything in your life. Change your beliefs, change your life, change your world.

<u>Examining Our Beliefs</u>

What are some beliefs that you had prior to this book about your students?

_____

_____

_____

_____

Upon further examination, do you still believe these to be the truth?

_____
_____
_____
_____
_____

Have you ever felt like someone's eyes lit up when they saw you? If so, how did it feel?

_____
_____
_____
_____
_____

Do your eyes light up when you look at your students? Do your students feel that you care about them/love them?

_____
_____
_____
_____
_____

How do you show your students that they are valued?

_____

_____

_____

_____

Have you experienced a "Grandma Pearl" or "Miss Pearl" in your life? If so, how did it impact your life and the way you felt about yourself and the world?

_____

_____

_____

_____

13
RELATIONSHIPS ARE KEY

Many years ago, when I taught third grade, one of my favorite times of the school day was when I would read aloud stories to my students. We all gathered together at the end of a long day to share a story. I would read the same stories to my classes every year and often dress up as the characters of our favorites for Halloween.

I usually read Roald Dahl's *Matilda* to the class, which is a story about a gifted young child who grows up with abusive, neglectful parents. In the story, Matilda's parents ignore her so badly that they almost forget that she exists. However, she is a magical genius, and spends her early childhood at the library teaching herself to read. Matilda survives because she starts to realize that she has wonderful, magical powers inside of her, and is a kind-hearted person even though her parents don't notice her at all. When she is old enough to enroll in school, she is noticed by a kind, young teacher, Miss Honey, who ends up adopting Matilda at the end of the story.

I read the book to the students because it involved magical powers, the love of reading, and a fun heroic victory over the evil villain, Ms. Trunchbull, who is defeated by Matilda and her magic. I chose the book because of the fun and magic and hadn't thought about the theme on a deeper level. But one of my students had a particularly difficult home life at the time. And this student was amazingly wonderful. She was kind, compassionate, and bright. I noticed she paid extra close attention as we read *Matilda*, so I started calling her "The Real-Life Matilda" because I thought she was a magical genius. For the rest of the school year, I called her Matilda, and so did the rest of the class.

After third grade, her beloved grandmother and her father died unexpectedly. Her life became even more difficult. Throughout the rest of her elementary years, I called her Matilda whenever I saw her because I honestly believed she was a magical genius, just like the character in the story.

Last year, I received a message from Matilda. She was all grown up and told me that she found her very own, real life Miss Honey. Her high school teacher had adopted Matilda into her own loving family. She also sent me a picture of her tattoo, which was the storybook character Matilda, and her new mother got a honeybee tattoo. She said she wanted to send me the picture of her Matilda tattoo because her story of hope, of being the real-life Matilda, started in the third grade.

I tell this story because I had no idea that loving my students and showing them how much I thought they were special could impact them. I didn't even know it at the time. I just loved my students and tried to create a loving, fun environment where they could learn and enjoy their childhood. I wanted them to experience joy at school. Many of my students experienced a lot of trauma for various reasons, and teachers and school had the power to be a bright light for them. I had no idea that believing in a child could help plant the seed of hope, allowing them to believe in themselves just as much.

Teachers are in powerful positions. Teachers have the power to be the difference makers in a child's life. Teachers can create a ripple effect that can change the world. And it doesn't take much. It simply takes the willingness to see them as the magical beings that they are and show them that you care.

How to Really Connect with Students

Kids learn from people who they think care about them, and they feel safe when they feel cared about. Relationships really mean love. Teachers have the power to instill the belief in students that they matter. Teachers can show students that they are valuable beings, that they are valued. Unfortunately, this works the other way as well. I have heard far too many stories about teachers whose apathy or criticism has scarred students. Apathy is the villain. Empathy is the hero.

Connection is what life and learning is truly about. Without connection and relationships, you can't do any of the other good stuff. Your kids have to trust you if you plan to lead them properly. Trust is a must, and kids know how to recognize fake. Just be your absolute most genuine human self.

Just as our brainstems protect us from harm and perceived threats, our egos do the same. I like to call our egos our "protective barriers." We all have them. We have developed our protective barriers over time, and sometimes they harden and thicken so much that they protect us from all the good and the potential bad. The scars of our protective barriers have thickened so much that none of our inner light can shine out of us and none of the light that others want to shine on us can get through. Brene Brown refers to this as our "shield of armor." This keeps us from feeling vulnerable to social threats, but it also keeps more of the good stuff out.

One of the beautiful things about children is that they haven't had as much time to develop their protective barriers. They are more real and genuine. They say what they mean and they mean what they say. They shine their light freely upon us all.

However, when children experience trauma and distress, they quickly form scabs over this pain and start forming their protective barriers very early. This shows up as kids who are very:

- Defensive
- Disrespectful
- Argumentative
- Oppositional
- Defiant
- Avoiders/don't listen to you-especially if you are lecturing or criticizing them.

From a brain science point of view, these students are always on high alert for danger and threats, both real and perceived. Their brains have become more vulnerable to stress because of their high levels of trauma. This means they will take more time to develop a connection and relationship with you. You are perceived as a *threat* because you are unfamiliar, even if you are kind. They need time to trust you and time to test you.

Here are some tips for connecting with your students:

1. Let down your armor. If you come in with your own armor and protective barriers wrapped around you tightly, there will be no way for the light of connection to pass from the vulnerable cracks in your barrier to their cracks in their barrier. In other words, your hearts will both be blocked, and you won't connect. Your job as the adult, the leader in charge, is to un-barrier yourself. Take that protective barrier down and let the child see your true light.

2. Be open and genuine, rather than trying to be perfect. You don't have to be perfect, because none of us are.

We often think we are the only ones who feel self-conscious sometimes. This isn't true. We are all self-conscious sometimes, and we are all threatened by unpredictability to a certain extent; it is part of our brain's way of keeping us safe from danger.

Let this down a bit with your students. Do it for their sake, and do it for your sake, because connection is what we are all here for, and we can only connect when we allow ourselves to be seen for who we are.

Kids are never going to be perfect. Even if they seem perfect, this could be a problem, a shield of perfectionism that they are using to be accepted and approved of. Let them be imperfect. Show them that you love them no matter what and that they don't have to be perfect. And then teach them the skills they need to know to learn and grow and live and spread kindness throughout the world. This is our job as educators.

3. Accept yourself for exactly who you are, flaws and all. Accept your students for who they are, flaws and all. Kids are just tiny humans. They are all doing their best to survive and live and navigate life. Sometimes they don't have as many supportive, loving adults in their lives as we assume they have. And sometimes this makes them act in ways that are difficult. They are testing us. They are trying to find out if we are safe people. Be the safe person. Sometimes you are the only one they have.

4. Stop lecturing. One of the most common things that I see and hear at high trauma, high stress schools is lecturing.

When students are "getting into trouble" repeatedly, breaking rules, getting in fights, and being disruptive, the first thing that usually happens is they get lectured. They get lectured by the teachers, principals, social workers, and counselors. The problem with this is they tune you out. They have heard it all before. They are just hearing one thing in these "lectures" and that is: "Authority figures think I am bad, therefore I must be bad."

I hear teachers and administrators and disciplinarians who are completely and utterly annoyed and dejected that the students "never listen" even after they have lectured them over and over on the same issue. This is because "lecturing" is disconnecting and disregarding. Think about a time where you have been lectured by an authority figure. What do you do? Most likely, you shut down and tune them out, just waiting for the humiliation to be over. It does NOT make you think, "I should listen to this person and take what they are saying to heart."

Instead, we need to listen. Listen to our students. Give them a safe space to talk and process their feelings. Let them know it is safe to talk. And then ask them what they need from you. Teach them how to regulate their emotions in a safer, better way. Listening is a skill that takes practice because most people don't listen. Instead, they are on alert, waiting to reply with what they "think" they are expected to say. You have to trust yourself and believe that who you are authentically is good enough and perfect enough. You do not have to have all the right answers when you are simply listening.

Each human being is a soul who wants connection. Everyone wants to be seen and heard and loved for exactly who they are. And we can't do that from a superior, "I know more than you" orientation because that's not true. On a soul level, we don't really know more or less. We all can feel the truth. It is just that our layers and layers of ego protection need to be peeled away so we can have a soul connection.

We are programmed to care about appearances and what people think of us as well as think we need to be in control when we're in leadership positions. Instead, acknowledging the truth and imperfections of a situation can be more connecting.

People who are great at communicating with children are able to drop their own egos and need for complete control. They have a way of being next to a child and letting them know that no matter what mistakes they make, the adult still believes in the child, and that the child is still lovable and a good, perfect human. These special individuals can help teach, coach and guide a student toward all the skills they need to become the person they are meant to become.

Recap on Great Communication with Traumatized and Non-Traumatized Students

1. Sit or walk next to them. Do not sit face to face or approach them directly, and do not demand that they make eye contact with you. This can be perceived as a threat.

2. Listen. Just listen. Try not to say anything at all. Usually, they will start talking when they feel safe enough to do so. Do not start interrogating or lecturing or saying anything that could be perceived as condescending. Do not initiate a power struggle by trying to get them to do anything they are resistant to doing.

3. It is important that you provide safety. This student is feeling unsafe and needs an adult to provide the safety of a space where they can become regulated.

4. Instead of trying to have "power over" a student, think about empowering them. Give the student space to think, feel and talk if they want to. Do not try to force anything.

5. If you are a principal, administrator, or person in charge of "discipline" in your school, do something active with the student. Remember to be beside them. Walking, coloring, playing with Play Doh, and doodling are all great activities, even for middle school or high school students. Work side by side, together, so the student feels safe with you, and understands that you are there together with them to support them in whatever it is they need to learn.

6. When the student is calm, they will probably start talking if they do not perceive you as a threat. If you have a history of lecturing or being condescending, it may take some apologizing on your part.

There is a printable version of this on my website at https://christinarenzelli.com/creatingcalm.

In my experience, everyone is stressed out in a school, especially in high trauma environments. Many teachers, administrators, staff and students are hanging on by a thread. Stress levels are through the roof, and most are living in survival mode.

When everyone is stressed out in a school, people don't think they have time for this kind of slow connection-building stuff. And usually, they don't. But it is time for us to make the time. Anyone who leads anyone needs to know how to do this.

Do not think you have to "punish" or "fix" the person. That is how connections get fractured. Shift your mind instead to:

- How can I connect with this person?

- How can I show them that I see them as a lovable, perfectly imperfect human, even though they made a (big) mistake?

- How can I show them that they are lovable and worthy despite and because of whatever challenges they are experiencing?

- How can I best serve this person? As their leader, you are there to serve them. Step aside from your ego for a moment and ask: "What does this person need the most right now?"

Usually, school discipline problems come from a disconnection. The person in power is trying to make the person in trouble "submit" to their power, and that is the opposite of connection, understanding and leadership. This says, "Your human-ness is less than mine," and nobody can connect or feel good with this kind of interaction. That elicits the natural defense mechanisms inside our brain and soul to fight, flee, or shut down and freeze.

Disconnection creates all sorts of problems because we humans are wired for connection. Many of us never learned how to authentically connect, or we forget because society encourages us to walk around inauthentically every day. People just rush around on autopilot, fearful of being seen or vulnerable, fearful of really connecting, living, and embracing our flawed humanness. Instead, we wear masks of perfection But while shame hurts, accepting and embracing our imperfections can be healing.

Reflection

Do you accept yourself as you are, flaws and all? If yes, in what ways do you show yourself acceptance?

_____
_____
_____
_____
_____

If you answered "no," how can you start to practice self-acceptance and embrace your imperfections to feel you are enough simply because you are human?

_____
_____
_____
_____
_____

How do you think that your Ego blocks you when you communicate with students or others? If so, what are some ways you can let down your "shield?"

_____
_____
_____
_____
_____

Do you accept your students as they are, flaws and all?

_____
_____
_____
_____
_____

What are some ways to be a "safe place" for your students when they need a safe place to land?

___

Prior to this book, were you a "lecturer" when it comes to "discipline?" If so, how did it feel to you?

___

Have you ever felt a student disengage when you needed to have an important discussion? If so, why do you think it happened?

___

How would you describe yourself as a listener?

_____
_____
_____
_____

Have you ever been fully listened to and acknowledged? If so, how did it feel?

_____
_____
_____
_____

What kind of listener do you want to be?

_____
_____
_____
_____

Did you have a Grandma Pearl or Miss Pearl in your life, like from the previous chapter? Who listened and believed in you? Or, who inspires you now as you look forward to growing your teaching career?

_____

_____

_____

_____

_____

14
TAKING CARE OF TEACHERS

<u>The Story of Ms. Johnston</u>

Ms. Johnston is a struggling 8th grade English teacher in her second year of teaching. She hasn't figured it all out yet, but she knows that the students bring a lot of pain and trauma to school with them. She is stressed out and looking for new positions for the next school year. Her dream was always to teach students in high trauma schools, but she feels defeated by the realities of the system. The veteran teachers have told her to "get out now," while she still has the chance and not to get stuck like they are. Now that they have so many years in, they feel there is no chance to change careers.

Ms. Johnston grew up in the neighborhood where she now teaches, and she had a life like her students, with similar traumas. But the stress of teaching was almost too much for her to take. As a new teacher, she was never really taught what to do. She had big dreams of changing lives, but the reality has been far different. She has taken most of her sick days already because her immune system doesn't know how to cope with the new germs combined with the lack of sleep caused by her mind not shutting off at night. Her anxious mind is in problem-solving mode and she doesn't know how to shut it off. She has been seeking help from her doctor, who prescribed medication. Her colleague suggested it was normal, and pretty much the only way teachers could cope.

She knew many teachers in the school who dedicated their lives to teaching. Their personal lives were put on hold because of their tireless dedication to work. They tried never to miss a day of school because they knew students needed their consistent, stable presence. For many students, teachers are their only consistent positive. Toxic stress, poverty, addiction, incarceration, violence, and trafficking were all common, familiar scenarios that students experienced as an everyday reality. These teachers knew this, and they knew that none of them truly deserved the "bad kid" labels they were given for simply developing the necessary survival skills to live in reality. To these teachers, their students were lovely, bright, genius, and sensitive souls. They needed their warmth, dedication, consistency, high expectations, and unrelenting belief that they were beautiful, kind, smart children, capable of changing the world for the better.

But this dedication did not come for free. There was a heavy price to pay for waking early day after day and surviving such a stressful environment. The energy of the trauma their students experienced clung to them and followed them to school every day. It was in the air. It mirrored back to their colleagues, who were also in it for the purpose, yet fizzling with the reality of burnout. It seemed survival engulfed them all. Every teacher was tired. Exhausted. Most of the teachers who started at the school didn't last more than a year or two, but others hung on. Something kept them there. Sometimes it was love and purpose, and sometimes it was scarcity and desperation, exhaustion, and stuckness. Ms. Johnson's story is the story of so many teachers.

At times, they felt ineffective in teaching the curriculum. The test scores usually showed failure, which was a slap in the face after such hard work from teachers and hardworking students.

The stress took physical tolls on the teachers: chronic colds, backaches, migraines, and plantar fasciitis. But by May, the love and commitment would kick back in, whispering to hang on one more year. Over the summer, the under-eye circles would fade and faces would lose their tired, haggard look until October, when the cycle would start all over again.

These dedicated teachers often feared the worst: becoming one of the elder, stuck, burned-to-a-crisp teachers. They feared being one of the ones who had started out with love, commitment, and a dream to change the world or teach their favorite subject to a new generation, but who had become disheartened and closed off by the tough, harsh realities of being a teacher and dedicating their lives and careers to changing a system that was stacked against them. These teachers gave up trying to change any systems and decided to get through instead. They decided to fend for themselves and survive. They lived in survival mode and were recognized by their bitter, negative comments and withering appearances. Every school had a few. They had missed the boat years ago, failed to jump ship before it was too late, and now were just surviving until retirement, a scenario that was unfair to them and especially unfair to the students they took as their prisoners.

These teachers were few, but well recognized.

Like most organizations, people were people: some were there for their own interests, some were there for a more spiritual reason, and some were there for a paycheck and to just get through the day until evening and weekend. Most people hadn't examined their higher purpose in the world, even though we all have one whether we know about it or not.

Unfortunately, this meant that in many urban, inner city schools, there was a high teacher turnover. Most of the teachers were brand new, inexperienced and didn't quite have their teaching skills mastered yet. They had desire, enthusiasm, heart and the will, but without experience and effective college preparation and training, they often lacked the skills. Most teacher prep programs lacked sufficient training.

The Calling to Make A Difference

I believe that educators are some of the best, most caring people on earth. It can be a thankless, self-sacrificing job at times, and I don't think the general public can ever understand how hard teaching can be. I truly believe that most educators go into teaching to make a difference in the world.

For some, this call is stronger than others. Maybe they are inspired by a teacher who made a difference in their life as a child. There are some teachers who have lost their spark for teaching. Maybe they never had the "spark" or experienced the "calling to teach" to begin with.

I almost quit teaching after my first year. I thought that I just wasn't "cut out for teaching." Sure, I had gotten tens of thousands of dollars into debt to become a teacher, but I knew that I couldn't risk ruining the lives of one more group of kids. I didn't want to do them a disservice by being a bad teacher. Somehow, I got talked into teaching again, and I never regretted it. After my first year of bumps and bruises, I learned from all my mistakes and became the best teacher I could be. It was amazing. I woke up every day knowing that it was my life's purpose to go to school and positively impact the lives of my students. My theory was:

- If I can serve, inspire, empower, and add value to the life of even just **one** student, then it is all worth it.

- I work for God, a higher purpose, and a higher power, and I work for my students. Nothing else was going to matter. The paperwork didn't matter, test scores didn't matter, appearances didn't matter. Nothing else mattered. I worked for my kids. It was going to be about the impact I could have on human lives, and that was it. Nothing else was really important. This simple philosophy cut a lot of the clutter and stress out of the parts of teaching that others found so stressful. I didn't worry so much if my lesson plans weren't perfect, and I could follow my students' curiosity rather than worrying about boring guidelines.

These two guidelines served me and my students very well for twelve years. I taught hundreds of students with the belief that it is all about the connection and love, and a calling to make a difference. Nothing else ever mattered. Ironically, our test scores were always great, even during my disastrous first year.

The First Step to Avoiding Teacher Burnout

Get Super Clear About Your Why.

This is the most important factor in teaching. Why are you an educator? Why did you become a teacher or administrator? Teaching is not for everyone. It takes a unique person to be an educator. It isn't for those who seek fame, fortune, recognition, or even appreciation at times.

List all of your reasons why you want to be an educator.

And after each reason, I want you to ask another why. For example:

My why:

I love helping people. Ok, Why? Because it makes me feel good to make a difference. Ok, why? Because I love seeing that people are happy and empowered. I love helping people see what strength they have inside of them and gain confidence. Why? Because when they feel confident, they can empower others, etc. It's a ripple effect.

See? I just found my true why. I love making a difference, helping people to empower themselves so they can empower others and create a ripple effect throughout the world and generations of humanity.

Everyone's why is different, so I would like you to find yours. This exercise is to make sure you are really in the right profession, because if you aren't:

- Your students will pay the price by having a teacher whose heart isn't really into it
- You will pay the price by being miserable
- Your family/friends/partner will pay the price by you being miserable
- Your true calling will pay the price by not having you to do what you genuinely want to do.

1. Why did you want to be an educator?

_____
_____
_____
_____
_____

2. Why is that important to you now?

_____

_____

_____

_____

3. Why? Why? Why?

_____

_____

_____

_____

So, for those of you who just figured out teaching isn't your true calling, congratulations on being honest with yourself! Did you know that up to 50% of teachers don't make it past the five-year mark? They did all the work, survived, and didn't come out in the end with a strong enough why to continue with the career path. You just saved yourself all of that torture, and now you can focus on what you would rather do instead of being stuck in a vital profession that requires a strong sense of purpose.

If you feel that teaching is not your true calling, I would be happy to have a conversation with you to help you figure out what is. I love assisting people in identifying and living their life purpose. Please reach out at https://christinarenzelli.com/contact-us.

For the rest of you, congratulations! You are going to change lives, or continue changing lives, and make the world a better place through your service as an educator. Teachers are life changing resilience builders, inspiring and empowering one student at a time. This profession is a true gift once we get past the learning curve, and there is no greater reward than changing and impacting a person's life forever.

Sometimes teachers find that their why is "I want to teach chemistry and change the world" or "I want to teach people to love singing" and so they focus on the content. This is ok, but you need to understand that you are teaching people first; then you can teach the subject matter. Without this, teaching will be even more difficult. If subject matter/passion is more important than the human, you will have difficulty teaching in a public-school setting, especially in a high trauma school setting.

Reflection

How does being an educator energize you?

_____

_____

_____

_____

How does being an educator drain your energy?

_____

_____

_____

_____

What is the most stressful part of your work? Why, Why, Why?

_____

_____

_____

_____

What are some things you can do to reduce your stress? Some people use exercise, even just a walk around the house or neighborhood, a bath, reading a book, taking a drive, taking a nap, meditating by focusing on breathing for a minute to fifteen minutes, etc. What are a few things you can choose for you?

_____

_____

_____

_____

_____

15

CREATING REGULATION PLANS TO REPLACE PUNITIVE SYSTEMS

Replacing punitive systems such as detentions, suspensions and expulsions with regulation plans can transform learning systems completely. The issue that I see is that a lot of school systems like to "test the water" with this "new way" but only do so half-heartedly. There are many reasons for this, but I have found that regulation plans work best when everyone is on board, receiving training and individual coaching to implement the new system. It also works best when "discipline" staff such as police officers, security guards, and detention monitors, are replaced with staff who are trained to help students regulate, understand the stress response, and teach them the skills of self-regulation

<u>Dysregulated Classrooms</u>

Energy snowballs. If there is one dysregulated person in the classroom, he or she can quickly cause those around them to start getting dysregulated. The classroom energy starts feeling chaotic and the teacher starts feeling stress because they are losing self-control. The teacher's stress response elevates, and they become dysregulated. When the teacher becomes dysregulated, the entire classroom will feel it and become dysregulated. It is the snowball effect.

Here is an example, but not from a classroom. Recently, I was meeting with a friend at a restaurant. The restaurant had several nook and cranny rooms, where people could go and eat. We were seated near a room with a big dining table. A pregnant woman sat with her two young children, estimated ages 5 and 3. I noticed her voice tone was high and anxious, and everything she said to her five-year old was loud and came across as angry. I don't think that was her intention, but I could tell she was getting stressed out. He became more and more dysregulated, and she became louder and louder, shouting at him and calling him bad. She began to threaten him with punishments, and he just got farther out of control and dysregulated. At one point, he ran out of the dining room and into the restaurant. My friend tried to carry on with our conversation, but I could feel my own stress response going up. The children were both crying and screeching, and the mother was upset and dysregulated. She didn't understand her own stress response, and because of that, she was escalating her kids' behavior because she was activating their stress response. She interpreted it as they were being "bad," and "brats." The five-year old's stress response was triggered, and he ran out, (flight). She chased after him and yanked his arm to get him back into the dining room.

This kind of stress response/tantrum/stressed out parenting and teaching happens every single day. But I am here to tell you:

1. That child (those children) did not want to "be bad." I am sure of it. They were just dysregulated and confused. They did not know how to regulate themselves at all.

2. The mother did not want to scream and yell at her children and yank their arms in public. She just didn't know how to regulate herself, and she certainly didn't know how to regulate her children.

How to regulate a dysregulated student:

1. RECOGNIZE THE WARNING SIGNS

What do you do if you encounter someone who is in the stress response? The stress response can also be called "throwing a fit," "losing one's temper," "out of control," "having a tantrum." You will most likely know that the person is dysregulated by some or more of the following signs:

- Seems upset: crying, shaking, etc.
- Seems angry: shouting, cursing, pacing, arguing, fighting, becoming defensive or offended
- Starts moving around more or can't be still
- Starts talking more than usual, or talking louder than the set tone for the situation
- Isolating, avoiding others, completely shuts down. At school, this happens when kids put their heads down or cover their faces. I've seen them seek out a corner to sit in and curl up in a ball, refusing to respond to anyone.
- Throwing things
- Swearing
- Leaving the classroom
- Hurting people or fighting
- Hurting one's self
- Sweating, singing, tapping or pounding fist or pencil, pacing, crying, squatting, bouncing legs, rocking
- Red face, heavy breathing,
- Getting noticeably quiet
- Damaging things, acting hyper, clenching teeth
- Being rude, or "unruly" (seeming disrespectful)

The truth is, everyone gets dysregulated, and it can look vastly different for us all. Recognizing these common warning signs is the first step to becoming a great "Regulator." It is also key to remember this:

***SIGNS OF DYSREGULATION ARE NOT NECESSARILY SIGNS OF "DISRESPECT**

I think that this is where traditional punitive behavior techniques go wrong. They assume that signs of dysregulation are just kids behaving "disrespectfully," and then the first thing that happens is that the adult in charge takes it personally. We take it PERSONALLY, as a sign of DISRESPECT, and then WE get dysregulated. This only escalates matters, and before too long the teacher and student (parent/child, boss/employee) are in a full-blown power struggle.

2. Now that you are noticing a student is becoming dysregulated, or is in full blown FEAR mode, what can you do, as the person in charge, to help them calm down, or de-escalate them?

This, of course, depends on many factors, including how many other people you are in charge of at the moment. During my work in schools as a coach, I had the luxury of being able to walk around in the hallways throughout the day, not being "in charge" of any students or a classroom. My job was to coach teachers and administrators. However, I am also a licensed teacher who happened to be trained in the neuroscience of trauma and stress, so when I would walk through the hallways and see a dysregulated student, I took the opportunity to use what I knew to help the student. In one case, there was a chaotic classroom with a substitute teacher, and one of the girls was so stressed she ran out into the hallway where a well-meaning hall monitoring teacher approached her and started yelling at her. She was doing what we are all trained to do: discipline. The problem at that time was, the student was already dysregulated from the chaos in her classroom, and the hall monitor's disciplinary, in-your-face, tough love approach was perceived as an extreme threat to the girl's already hypersensitive stress response system and she reacted in FIGHT mode. I will not repeat here what the girl said to the teacher, but she looked like she was going to hit her and get in major trouble, but also potentially injure the teacher. I stepped in and de-escalated the situation. Here is what I did.

First, I stepped BESIDE the student. Never get in someone's face when they are in the stress response. This is what the teacher was doing. This is a major threat to anyone and everyone. Instead, I stood next to her, and said, "Let's take a walk, come on." The other key here, was to use a very calm and quiet voice, unlike the voice of the hall monitor, who was yelling and trying to be authoritative. I just said, "Come on, lets go for a walk." Now, if I were a total stranger, the girl would not have gone with me. But instead she had seen me around the school, and thought I was a friendly, nonthreatening person. Therefore, she agreed to escape the scene with me and go for a walk.

I chose walking for two reasons. First, it is PHYSICAL, and movement can calm a dysregulated person. Secondly, we would be side by side for an extended period of time. This allowed the student to feel supported. Being side by side is essential to regulating a person because they are not feeling confronted, and instead feel like there's "someone to walk beside them."

I stayed QUIET as we walked. This was NOT the time to lecture, criticize or interrogate the student. When a person is in the stress response mode, they do not have full access to the cortex, the thinking part of their brain. Their brain is in survival mode, and that is what they are focused on. Their only focus is to get away from the perceived danger. We walked in silence, at least for a while. My silence conveyed that I WAS NOT A THREAT. This silence was the key. It helped calm her down, and as we walked, she started talking and talking. I don't even remember what she talked about, but she was thinking out loud, starting to process the events that had just taken place. As we walked and walked, she calmed down and started feeling safe. I did not have to lecture her or tell her anything. She just needed an adult to be there for her who wasn't going to add more threat. And I listened. By the end of our walk, I asked her what she might like to do differently, and she said she wanted to apologize to the hall monitor. It was HER idea, not mine. We went together to talk to the hall monitor, who she could now see, with her rational brain, was not a threat.

Later, in the following days and weeks, we talked about what had happened. I knew that the student needed to learn self-regulation skills, so I explicitly taught her.

1. What was happening in her brain when she had the stress response? I taught her that we are wired to guard ourselves against potential danger, and she must have sensed danger for her body and brain to react in that way. What was the perceived danger?

2. What kinds of things might trigger her?

3. What did she feel was happening in her body and mind when she started feeling dysregulated? I wanted her to start understanding how to recognize the feelings.

4. Once she recognized the feelings, what things could she do INSTEAD of reacting as she had?

5. I worked with her teachers, and we supported her in "practicing" the self-regulation techniques. Self-regulation, like all other skills, does not happen perfectly right away, but each time she practiced, she became more self-aware and was able to self-regulate rather than react. She learned to stay regulated most of the time. And she learned what her own personal triggers were, which empowered her to be more aware of her own stress response, allowing her to regulate and take care of her needs, rather than react in a way that would hurt herself, hurt others, and get her into trouble.

This school had a traditional discipline system, rather than what I'd like to call a "regulation system." Students who got in fights, or were considered disruptive, were punished by detentions or suspensions. This creates further problems, because students are "thrown out" and disregarded instead of being taught the skills they need to learn to control their impulses and stress response. THIS IS THE FUNDAMENTAL FLAW IN PUBLIC EDUCATION. I believe it is our job to teach kids the skills they need to self-regulate and stay present in school so they can learn and grow and thrive. But instead, many schools punish the behavior rather than teaching the skills that we all need to know to control our stress response and emotions.

It is also KEY to give them space to PRACTICE these skills. It is time that we take the shame out of the stress response. Let's shed the light on this, because it affects everyone. The more we bring it out into the open, rather than just assuming people are "bad" for not knowing about it, the easier it is to have empathy for each other.

Recap of Key Points

1. Recognize warning signs of dysregulation.

2. Do NOT take it personally, or as a sign of disrespect. It is the brain's protective mechanism.

3. Get BESIDE the person, not face to face. Stand beside with your support.

4. Give them SPACE. Do not try to talk or interrogate. Listen to them, as they will probably start processing out loud whatever triggered their dysregulation.

5. Once they are calm, you can ask questions.

6. Talk about what they could do instead next time, and ways they can STAY regulated rather than letting things get dysregulated.

7. PRACTICE. This is the key. Help them to practice scenarios where they might get dysregulated, and practice self-regulation techniques. It's all about PRACTICE, rather than perfection. We grow and learn the more we practice, make mistakes, and then have the freedom to learn and grow from our mistakes.

Reflection

Have you ever thought that a dysregulated student was being purposefully disrespectful to you?

_____
_____
_____
_____

Has this chapter or book shifted your perspective on "disrespectful" behaviors?

_____
_____
_____
_____

Components of a "Regulated Environment"

To maintain a calm, safe learning environment, there are several essential factors that I look for when coaching teachers. They are:

1. Routines, procedures and predictability

The brain feels safe when it knows what to expect. Predictable routines and procedures take the guesswork and uncertainty out of the situation, so the brain is able to relax a bit and be less on alert for danger.

2. Respect

Students need to feel respected and loved in order to learn.

3. Natural Rewards

Humans love to do things that feel rewarding. Often, I'll see teachers giving points, candy or objects as rewards, when a natural reward works so much better. By natural rewards, I mean things like a nice note, an acknowledgement, "eyes lighting up," or reading a story we can connect to on a deep level. Basically, anything that adds connection and fun will feel rewarding.

4. Movement and Rhythm

The brain and body need movement and rhythm to stay regulated. Rhythm can be music, tapping, jumping, or adding rhymes or songs into the lessons. The more rhythm and movement that is weaved into the lesson and day, the more regulated and happy the students will be.

5. Connection and Relationships

Students need to have strong relationships with their teachers, and they need to have a chance to cultivate relationships with their peers. Often, schools discourage talking or connecting among students to stay strict with the academics, but the more they can connect and work together, the more regulated they will be. It also cuts down on having to try to "control" them and prevent them from talking and connecting, which is natural for us to all seek connection.

6. Ownership

When the content you teach is relevant to students' lives and situations, and when students understand and agree to classroom expectations, they will have a sense of ownership in their learning. This creates a sense of empowerment.

Please go to https://christinarenzelli.com/creatingcalm for printable versions of this so you can easily reference this information.

16

CONCLUSION

I will leave you with my best advice from 12 years of teaching 3rd grade. I wrote this list on the evening of my very last day of school as a teacher.

1. Routines and organization are key to managing people, deadlines, and chaos.
2. Every person wants to be recognized, appreciated, and heard.
3. Most social problems happen because of a lack of empathy and communication.
4. Natural curiosity can be everything.
5. Don't aim for perfection, just do the best you can.
6. Small acts of kindness and recognition can transform the world.
7. Don't try to put people into boxes.
8. Everyone is different, but the same.
9. When things start to get overwhelming or boring, taking a break works like magic.
10. Boredom can be toxic or used as a sign to make a change. Choose either to be stuck or to take the sign that it's time to evolve.
11. Nothing is really that serious. Making things fun can be magic.
12. Don't even worry about what the other teachers are doing. Share ideas and ask for help but follow your own plan by being tuned in to the needs of your individual students.
13. If you lose sleep over it, you need a vacation.

14. Don't give anything or anyone all of your energy. Balance it.
15. Write it down. Just put it on a list and get to it when you get to it.
16. 90% of things aren't emergencies, but people will try to make you think they are.
17. The only important things are the ones that truly affect people. Standardized tests aren't really important, but friendship and enjoying reading are vital. Don't let the powers in charge make you define your priorities.
18. If there's no enjoyment in something, it's probably a waste of time.
19. When you have the freedom to choose what you want to read, you will become an amazing reader.
20. Take walk breaks around the school during your lunch break, or in circles around the room whenever you get a few minutes. Small changes/habits add up to make a huge impact.
21. Don't waste: time, money, or energy on junk that's really not important to you or anyone.
22. Most people don't remember your mistakes as long as you're honest, mean well, and take responsibility.
23. Less really is more. Simplify to improve. The simplest way is usually the best way, but simple is not necessarily easy.
24. Kids are people. Listen to them and talk to them like you would talk to any other human that you respect. No baby talk. Show them you understand.
25. Sometimes you have to cut corners. Let this set you free.
26. Connection is the key to it all.

Please go to https://christinarenzelli.com/creatingcalm for printable versions of this so you can easily reference this information.

Notes

Notes

Notes

Notes

Notes

ABOUT THE AUTHOR

Christina Renzelli is a Transformational Coach who works with clients to create their ideal professional and personal lives. She guides her clients through transformations in business, careers, relationships, and life as they partner to clarify priorities, remove obstacles and limiting beliefs, and achieve success.

She began her professional career as an English language teacher overseas and continued her teaching career in the USA. After more than fifteen years of teaching and a life-altering experience, she decided to reinvent herself and help more people live truer to the goals and dreams they have been putting off in their own lives. Having previously created a business as a professional organizer in which she helped clients declutter their homes, she realized that her true passion has always been coaching and guiding individuals and organizations in creating greater structure and identifying opportunities to transform and excel. She believes that everyone has special talents, skills, and unique gifts to be shared with the world. She peels away the layers of her clients' stories with non-judgmental listening and truth-telling exploration so that they can hear the voice of their own wisdom, intuition and truth.

Christina Renzelli, M.Ed, ACC is an ICF Certified Coach. She received her coach training through the Core Essentials Program at Coach University, a Master's Degree in Teaching and Learning from DePaul University in Chicago, Illinois, and a Bachelor's Degree in Linguistics from Ohio University.

Christina is also the author of *Organize Your Life: How to Find Clarity From Within.*

Made in the USA
Middletown, DE
12 May 2023

29914975R00080